Love, Acceptance & Forgiveness

Jerry Cook
with
Stanley C. Baldwin

GL Regal Books A Division of G/L Publications
Glendale, California, U.S.A.

Other good Regal reading:
Your Spiritual Gifts Can Help Your Church Grow,
    by C. Peter Wagner
Be a Leader People Follow,
    by David L. Hocking
Your Church Can Grow,
    by C. Peter Wagner
Your Church Has Real Possibilities,
    by Robert H. Schuller
The Power of a Loving Church,
    by Margaret and Bartlett Hess

The foreign language publishing of all Regal books is under the direction of GLINT. GLINT provides financial and technical help for the adaptation, translation and publishing of books in more than 85 languages for millions of people worldwide.

For more information write: GLINT, 110 W. Broadway, Glendale, CA 91204.

Scripture quotations in this publication are from *(NIV) The New International Version,* Holy Bible. Copyright © 1978 by New York International Bible Society. Other versions quoted are *The Living Bible (TLB),* copyright © 1971 by Tyndale House Publishers, Wheaton, Illinois. Used by permission; and the Authorized King James Version *(KJV).*

Second Printing, 1979

Published by Regal Books Division, G/L Publications
Glendale, California 91209
Printed in U.S.A.

Library of Congress Catalog Card No. 79-63763
ISBN 0-8307-0654-2

Contents

Dedicated to the patient, loving, and adventurous people who have really written these pages—my brothers and sisters comprising the East Hill Church.

Preface

The nature of Christ's church on this planet is of consuming interest to me not just because I am a pastor, but because I am also a part of that church. I am in the process of pastoring my first church. That process has stretched over the past 14 years, and will stretch considerably further. My wife and I wanted a place to invest our lives; the Lord gave us enough for several lifetimes.

I came directly from seminary, and my wife from teaching to our tiny church of 23 people. We were equipped to answer all questions and forge into new streams of Christian thought, supposedly. We discovered we really knew nothing about our task. I had not come to grips with the nature of the true church of Christ.

We were driven by our congregation to face with them the implications of being truly Christian in a non-Christian, and at times anti-Christian, world.

That adventure led us into the lives and homes of all

7

sorts of people. We began to sense the thrill of the Jesus-life effectively invading and challenging every area of human hurt. From the confusion of the drug culture to the violence of the street and motorcycle gangs, to the sophisticated offices of the executive set, and everything in between, we saw the church function.

Suddenly, divorce was not merely a theological workshop but the heartbroken and disillusioned person sitting across the table. Drugs were not only a social evil, but the blank and tortured faraway look that makes a teenager suddenly an old person.

We began to understand that the church was people— real people—changed by the power of Christ, filled with the Spirit of Christ, touching the hurting, dying and cynical modern man with the life of Jesus Himself. "The church which is His body, the fullness of Him . . ."

This book presents some of the viewpoint and perspective that we have learned together as a group of people serious about truly being His Body. It is written for the church—pastors, homemakers, taxi drivers, executives, blue collar, white collar, or no collar. It is a sincere effort to share with you the sheer excitement that exists in being "the church."

I have found in Stan Baldwin a sensitive and perceptive writer. His questions, observations and balance have given to this book that which I alone could never have hoped to achieve. He has waded through hours of tapes and stacks of materials and has compiled those things we truly believe.

If in the reading of this you are called upon to question, evaluate, or even change your thinking, so be it. What I desire is that all of us who go by the name Christian be effectively living out the implications of that name. It is time to get the church into the world and so fulfill the "Immanuel principle"—God with us.

one

A Place Where People Are Made Whole

A pastor in our town whom I knew only slightly became involved in adultery. As a result, his marriage went on the rocks and his ministry was destroyed. Since he was a strong Christian leader in our area, this brother's fall came with a resounding crash. His church splintered into a dozen fragments and hurting, confused people were scattered all over the city.

A year and a half after all that happened, I received a phone call at 7:30 A.M. one Sunday. It was this former pastor. He said, "Would you mind if my wife and I came to church this morning?"

I said, "Why would you even call and ask that question? Of course we wouldn't mind."

"Well," he said, "you know this is my second wife and I am divorced from my first. Are you aware of this?"

I said, "Sure, I'm aware of it."

"Well," he said, "I'll tell you, Jerry, we've been trying

for eight months now to find a place to worship. The last time we tried was a month ago. That morning we were asked from the pulpit to leave. We've been met at the door of other churches by pastors who heard that my wife and I were coming. They asked us not to come in, said we would cause too much trouble. Still others have heard that we might show up and called in advance to ask us please not to come."

He said, "Frankly, I don't think we could handle it again if we were to come and be an embarrassment to you and be asked to leave. I just don't know what would happen; my wife is close to a nervous breakdown." By now he was weeping. "I know that you have video for overflow crowds," he said. "If you want you can put us in a room where no one will see us and let us watch the service."

I said, "Listen, you be there and I'll welcome you at the door."

He came with his wife and their little baby. They came late and sat in the back.

The compounding thing was that many of the people who had been hurt through his fall were now a part of our congregation. Nevertheless, we extended fellowship to that man and the Lord did a cleansing and a healing. We shed so many tears together. I never will forget how he grabbed me and buried his head on my shoulder, a man 15 to 20 years my senior. He wept like a baby and held to me like a drowning man. He said, "Jerry, can you love me? I've spent my life loving people but I need someone to love me now."

In the weeks and months that followed, he met with our elders regularly and wept his way back to God through a most intense, sometimes utterly tearing repentance. If ever in my entire life I've seen godly sorrow for sin, I saw it in that man. He literally fell on the floor before our elders, grabbed their feet and implored them, "Brothers, can you ever forgive me?"

God healed that man and restored him to wholeness. Today, he's back in the ministry.

I say to you, that brother was restored only because God enabled us to love and accept and forgive him. Love, acceptance, forgiveness—those three things are absolutely essential to any ministry that will consistently bring people to maturity and wholeness. If the church is to be the force for God in the world that it should be, it must learn to love people, accept them and forgive them.

The church is in the world to minister salvation to people. The word *salvation* in its broadest sense means to bring to wholeness. It's interchangeable with the word *healing*. We read, "And the prayer of faith shall save the sick" (Jas. 5:15, *KJV*). The same Greek word rendered *save* here is translated *heal* elsewhere. (The *NIV* says, "Will make the sick person well.")

Within the community of the gathered church, then, people need to be saved, healed, brought to wholeness in every area of their lives. But before there can be a coming to wholeness, certain guarantees must be made to people. Otherwise they will not risk themselves to be open with us enough to receive healing.

The minimal guarantee we must make to people is that they will be loved—always, under every circumstance, with no exception. The second guarantee is that they will be totally accepted, without reservation. The third thing we must guarantee people is that no matter how miserably they fail or how blatantly they sin, unreserved forgiveness is theirs for the asking with no bitter taste left in anybody's mouth.

If people are not guaranteed these three things, they will never allow us the marvelous privilege of bringing wholeness to them through the fellowship of the church.

Love One Another

"We know that we have passed from death to life, because we love our brothers. Anyone who does not love remains in death" (1 John 3:14). According to this Scripture, the evidence that we're children of God is our love for other believers. If love is lacking we "remain in death." We are not the sons and daughters of God, no matter what experience we claim in the past. Now that is both frightening and liberating. I know that I have passed from death unto life. How do I know it? Well, there was that time I got down on my knees ... No, that's not good enough. I know I'm a child of God because I love.

That's not some theological or philosophical statement. I actually do love the brethren, and that is evidence of God's Spirit living in me. You see, in the natural I don't love anybody. My personal history is one of exploitation and manipulation of other people. But now I love them. Therefore, I know I am a child of God; my daily experience verifies it.

Today the church of Jesus Christ needs to make a bold commitment to love people and then dedicate itself to fulfilling that commitment. Our whole life-style should tell people, "If you come around here, we're going to love you. No matter who you are or what you've done or how you look, smell or behave, we're going to love you."

We must remember that the word for love here is *agape*. *Agape* love first exists, then it affects the emotions. For God so loved the world that He sat in heaven and had warm feelings? No, that's nonsense. God so loved the world that He gave. That's it! *Agape* is a volitional commitment to another that motivates us to

12

act on his behalf. Every time you find a corresponding action to the concept of *agape*, it is a giving action.

Furthermore, *agape* involves the kind of giving that cannot be compensated. That concept of love is quite foreign to our culture. The mentality of this world leads us to love and give only when there is reason to assume that our love will be reciprocated. This reciprocity is tested carefully during a "getting acquainted" time. If things look promising, if our approach meets with acceptance and response, we risk a bit further and a friendship is established.

In the Kingdom of God we first love, then we move into acquaintance. In this world we first get acquainted, then we move into love sometimes. As a result, most people have many acquaintances and a few friends but they are dying from lack of love.

Love is commitment and operates independently of what we feel or do not feel. We need to extend this love to everyone who comes into our church: "Brother, I want you to know that I'm committed to you. You'll never knowingly suffer at my hands. I'll never say or do anything, knowingly, to hurt you. I'll always in every circumstance seek to help you and support you. If you're down and I can lift you up, I'll do that. Anything I have that you need, I'll share with you; and if need be I'll give it to you. No matter what I find out about you and no matter what happens in the future, either good or bad, my commitment to you will never change. And there's nothing you can do about it. You don't have to respond. I love you, and that's what it means."

A church that can make that commitment to every person is a church that's learning to love and a church that will be a force for God.

Sometimes when I am speaking, I select an individual from the group whom I do not know. I express the

13

forever love commitment to him personally before everyone. I do it for effect but it is also my sincere commitment to that person.

One of these people came to me several years later and reminded me of the commitment I had made to him. In fact, he repeated it to me almost word for word. "I've been up all night in anticipation of talking to you," he continued. "I have to tell you that I've blown it." He then proceeded to describe the chaos in his life, his marriage and his ministry. As his shocking story unfolded, I found myself becoming angry and disgusted with him for blighting the name of Jesus and forfeiting his ministry so foolishly. *Dear God, I thought, what have I gotten myself into? Can I really keep my commitment to this man? When he's all done pouring himself out to me, can I totally accept him and not think any less of him?* I was not at all sure I could.

But while he was speaking, a strange thing happened. God gave me compassion for the man. When he was through I said, "What you have told me is probably the most disgusting, despicable thing I can think of. I don't know of anything more you could have done to make me reject you. You've left no stone unturned. But you need to know that the Holy Spirit is giving me the capacity to love you. And because I love you, and that love has been placed in my heart by the Holy Spirit, God loves you and offers you complete forgiveness."

It was just like turning on a faucet the way the man began to weep. Then he prayed. On the basis of my love he asked God to forgive him. The outworking of all that over a period of time brought about the restoration of his home and his ministry, and now he is serving Christ.

That man, to this day, is one of the most blessed people in my thinking. I love him more now than when I first made that commitment to him, in spite of what he went through, even though what I found out was shocking to me. But he had to tell someone. And because I had made that commitment to him, he felt he could come to me. You see, he was at a point emotionally where he could not risk rejection but neither could he keep silent. Like many other hurting people, he desperately needed someone to love him and had almost nowhere to turn. No wonder a church that knows how to love becomes a force for God.

Acceptance—Love in Action

A woman came to me one day and said she'd have to stop having Bible studies in her home.

"That's too bad," I said. "Why?"

"People are coming and smoking in our house," she replied.

"So?" I asked, puzzled.

"It's stinking up our new drapes," she said.

I was beginning to get the picture. "Do you want sterile drapes," I asked, "or do you want to expose hurting people to the love of Jesus?"

Love means accepting people the way they are for Jesus' sake. Jesus hung around with sinners and if we're too holy to allow people to blow smoke in our faces, then we're holier than Jesus was. He didn't isolate Himself in the synagogue. In fact, He mixed with sinners so much that the self-righteous got upset about it. "He's friendly with some very questionable people," they said. And Jesus replied, "Yes, because I didn't come to minister to you religious leaders. I came to call sinners to repentance."

Isn't that fantastic? Jesus spent His time with dirty, filthy, stinking, bent sinners. And when those kind of people find someone who will love and accept them, you won't be able to keep them away.

Why do they go to the bar? They're looking for someone who will listen to them. So they get drunk and blow all their problems out on the bartender. He cries along with them and laughs along with them. Then he says, "OK, it's two o'clock, go on home." So they stagger out and are back the next night for the same thing. What are they looking for? They're looking for love and acceptance. But they can't come to the church because the church doesn't like drunks.

A young man phoned me early one morning and said, "I'm going to commit suicide."

I said, "Why are you talking to me?"

He said, "Because I don't want to do it but I don't know what else to do. I'm a heroin addict, and last night I nearly killed a man." He told me the circumstances, how he'd been stopped from killing this man. He said, "I'm afraid to go home. I'm afraid to do anything. I'm totally out of control and the only thing I know to do is end my life."

I asked him if we could get together. "No way," he said. "I called a pastor a few months ago and he told me to come by his office. When I got there, he had the sheriff waiting to pick me up. I spent the next six months in jail. I made up my mind then I wasn't about to go to another creep preacher."

My heart broke. What could I do? I said, "Look, I'll go to my office right now. Give me 15 minutes. Then you drive by the church until you're satisfied that no one else is around. I'll stay there for three hours. If at any time during those three hours you want to risk coming in, I'll be the only one there."

I waited at the church two and a half hours. Finally I heard the front door open, then a knock on my office door. I let him in. He gave his life to Christ right there. It was a powerful, beautiful kind of thing. The heart-breaking question is, why hadn't he found love and acceptance before in the one place on earth that's supposed to know how to love?

I know churches that have split because "long hairs" have come in. Pastors and elders who are afraid of long hair and bare feet are in the wrong business.

"But what will sister-so-and-so think?"

Does it really matter? The church should state, "We're going to love and accept people, and if you don't want to love people, you're in the wrong place. Because this church is going to love people."

Unreserved acceptance of people should be a habit with us. There's no other way to get close enough to people to help them at the level of their deepest needs. When we cultivate the habit of accepting people, they open up to us, they like us, they trust us instinctively.

I was at the county courthouse getting a passport one day when I spotted a young couple I recognized as being from our church. I asked what they were doing and discovered they were getting a marriage license. "Well, Pastor," the young man said, "we've been shacking up for about four years now, and we figured we might as well do it right. Say, I forgot to bring anyone along. Would you mind being a witness for us?"

Now, this young man does not have a particularly soft voice, and there were about 25 people in that office. For some reason the whole room suddenly became very quiet. I felt that every eye in the place was on me, a pastor who had just been identified as knowing young couples who were shacking up together. What was I to do? Say to the fellow, 'Shh-shh, don't let anybody hear you"? Or give a little sermon of rebuke just so everyone would know I disapproved?

"Hey, that's fantastic," I said. "You're getting married!" And I signed as a witness.

17

I accepted that brother. The point is, though, I had accepted him long before this encounter and my acceptance was so solid that he wasn't afraid to tell me the truth now. I praise the Lord for that, because I can remember a day in my ministry when a person in his situation seeing me in there would have slipped away to come back only after I was gone.

Because we are accepted in the Beloved, we must be accepting of the beloved. I can't give up on you till God does, and He won't! We're safe with God, and we've got to be safe with one another. I've got to be safe with my brothers and sisters. I've got to be able to know that I can blow it and still be loved.

I'm only human, and you have no idea how human I am. You little realize the weakness and the frailty of the man who lives in this frame. But I know; I contend with it every day. I'm just mud, as you are. I've got to be able to fail and still be loved and accepted—by my wife, by my children, by my parishioners, by my parents. I simply cannot live with rejection. And that's not because I'm on an ego trip but because I'm a person.

Acceptance Is Not License

Earlier, I told about a fallen pastor who was restored to fellowship because he found love, acceptance and forgiveness at East Hill. What I did not tell you is that a barrage of phone calls began coming to us at that time from irate pastors and people. They were terribly upset that our accepting him would be interpreted as license for what he had done. I suppose that is possible. Perhaps some people would be so blind. But they would be wrong to make that assumption. We were neither countenancing his sin nor trying to be noble and heroic in bucking the tide of sentiment against him. We were simply and plainly loving him.

A leading church official called me during this time. He asked, "Do you know what you've done?"

I assured him that I most likely did not.

"Well," he said, "you've opened your doors to every broken-down pastor with ethical problems there is."

My answer to that is, "Praise the Lord. If they can't come here, where can they go? Where do we refer them? If people can't be healed in our congregation, where should we send them? Someone has to be the end of the line for messed-up humanity. We are not in a popularity contest."

Jesus was crucified at the end of His ministry, and it was the equivalent of the local ministerial association that put Him on the cross. The religious community may put you on the cross too. If so, pray that God will forgive them, for they know not what they do. The very brothers who would crucify you may also fall some day, and when they do, they should be able to come to you and find love, acceptance and forgiveness. They should find a welcome and hear a voice saying, "Brother, I know you are hurting. In Jesus' name, come in."

Never labor under the misconception that such acceptance breeds license. To the contrary, your very acceptance of a brother will make him strong. It will never confuse him in questions of right and wrong if your teaching and personal life-style establish clear standards. For example, a person who uses profanity is not going to imagine you approve of such language just because you accept him personally. As he hears your reverent speech and learns God's Word and, most important, comes to love God, he will understand clearly that profanity is wrong. But if you communicate personal rejection to such a person, he will never be around long enough to be touched by God through you.

The same principle applies in all our relationships

with other people. Jesus accepts us though we have much in our lives that offends His holiness. His acceptance of us does not imply approval of our unworthy behavior. If, then, we are acceptable to Jesus, who do we think we are to reject others?

Forgiveness—To Stop Playing God

"Be kind and compassionate to one another, forgiving each other, just as in Christ God forgave you" (Eph. 4:32).

I like Catherine Marshall's concept of forgiveness as she develops it in her book *Something More*. She suggests that forgiveness is releasing another from your own personal judgment. Taking your personal judgment off a person doesn't mean you agree with what he has said or done. It simply means you will not act as his judge. You will not pronounce a guilty verdict on him.

"But he was wrong," you say.

OK, but he's not standing under my judgment. I release him.

To keep another under your personal judgment is to play God with him. The Word says, " 'It is mine to avenge; I will repay,' says the Lord" (Rom. 12:19). And because He's going to repay, I don't have to.

"But that person hurt me, Lord. Did you know that?"

"Of course."

"Well, are you going to do anything about it?"

"What do you think?"

"Are you going to strike him dead?"

"Probably not."

"But, Lord . . ."

"Do you want to play God? If so, remember this: The moment you step in to bring judgment onto that man, you will come under my judgment."

Forgive, and you'll be forgiven. Judge not, and you'll

not be judged. That's in the Word (see Luke 6:37). Release people from your personal judgment! For unless I can be assured of your forgiveness, I cannot really open myself to you. You see, I know that sooner or later I will disappoint you and fail you. Not by design or desire, but I am imperfect; I'm still under construction. I must know that you will not condemn me when my weaknesses and flaws and sins begin to show. I need the assurance of your forgiveness—a forgiveness with no bitter aftertaste.

Remember, you are not the Lord. None of us is to function as Lord in anybody's life, ever, under any circumstances. There's only one Lord, and that's Jesus Christ. A pastor must never relate to his people as a lord. Pastors are not obligated to get people to heaven. That's the work of Jesus. A pastor's obligation to people is first to love and accept and forgive them, and second, to *bring them to ministry readiness by teaching them to do the same.*

This reduces things to such simplicity. Pastors are free to love their people. They don't have to be guardians. They are not wardens of the flock but shepherds of the flock. There's a big difference, and it's the difference between loving and judging.

When love, acceptance and forgiveness characterize our lives and our churches, the Lord will send us people who need to be made whole. A pastor friend called me one day very upset at our church. This was a brother I liked and respected then, and still do. He was irritated because some of his people had started coming to our church. I knew what he was talking about and I felt he needed to get it off his chest, so I let him talk. At one point he said, "You know what you are out there? You're nothing but a bunch of garbage collectors."

As I thought about it, I realized he was telling the

21

truth. That's exactly what we are, garbage collectors. What were we before Jesus found us? Weren't we all just garbage? Jesus finds us and recycles us.

I mentioned this in church one Sunday and afterward a man who owns a garbage collection agency came floating up the aisle, all excited. "That's super," he said. "Let me tell you something about garbage. There's a landfill near here. For 10 years we used it as a place to dump trash and garbage. Know what's there now? A beautiful park."

I've seen human garbage become beautiful too. I've seen the stench of sin turned into the fragrance of heaven. That's our business. We can't worry about what critics think or say. Where is God going to send the "garbage" for recycling if He can't put it on our doorstep? He'll find a place. If we're not open for business, someone else will be. But we want to be used of God.

When love, acceptance and forgiveness prevail, the church of Jesus Christ becomes what Jesus was in the world: a center of love designed for the healing of broken people, and a force for God.

two

The Need for a Guiding Philosophy

One thing working all kinds of devastation in the life of the church is the failure of the leadership to have a solid philosophy—a well-defined concept of how a church ought to operate and why. In the absence of such a philosophy, pastors tend to do one of three things: (1) they pastor from crisis to crisis; (2) they pick up on the current fad; (3) they simply subscribe to a concept of church life handed down to them.

Crisis to Crisis
A great deal of a pastor's life can be spent rushing from crisis to crisis so that he never has the opportunity to sit down and think through the question, "What in the world am I really in existence for anyway?"

It's easy to be trapped by the pressure of a moment.

Pastors find themselves thrown into situations and they have to deal with what's there. Problems arise in the personal lives of the people. Someone passes away, for instance, so the pastor quickly prepares a sermon about death. Or maybe there has been a major accident. The people involved were Christians, so questions arise about the sovereignty of God. The pastor quickly works up a message on the sovereignty of God.

Problems arise in the groups that comprise each congregation. Maybe one of the girls in the youth group has gotten in trouble; she's pregnant, an unwed mother-to-be. Parents are upset and the kids are asking questions. The result is a crisis in the youth department, and the pastor must step in and respond to the situation.

Next there's trouble with the church board. The church is buying property. Suddenly it becomes apparent that the congregation is party to a totally inadequate contract. The church is overcommitted and under-financed. Now the pastor must run to that crisis.

Problems arise in performing the pastoral duties themselves. "Oh, boy, here it is Friday evening already and I've hardly started to prepare my Sunday morning message—to say nothing of Sunday evening. What in the world am I going to do?" It's another crisis.

Stop!

Ask one question: Is a pastor to spend his entire life on call as a spiritual ambulance, or is there something more fundamental he should be doing?

One basic premise in my own philosophy of the church is that the people themselves are the ministers. When a crisis arises, it doesn't necessarily have to come to the pastor's office. When someone passes away, to stick with a foregoing example, the situation does not call for a theological treatise. It calls for people who understand the nature of grief and bereavement to move

24

in and, in a servant way, meet the personal needs of the sorrowing.

You see, it is not the pastor's job to meet everybody's need. It is the pastor's job to see that everybody's need is met. That is the difference between facilitating ministry and just running an ambulance service. The pastor should be a facilitator.

But we must have a basic health plan underlying all that, and that's where the pastor needs to be coming from. Two things are necessary: people must be trained to use their own gifts in ministry; and the church must grant the people the right to minister in crisis situations on the spot.

Crises cannot be avoided. They cannot even be scheduled. When a marriage blows up, someone's heart is breaking and the whole situation is about to go up in smoke, we can't say, "Well, let's see now, the pastor can see you a week from next Tuesday at 4:00 P.M." But we can involve people in ministry to the point that needs are met and the pastor is free of a constant demand to intervene in crises.

Church Fads

Another frightening result of not having a solid philosophical base for what we're doing is that our tendency then is to pick up on whatever is the going thing at the moment. We then pursue that until something comes along that looks better.

Several years ago, the Jesus movement hit the street. Suddenly it was everybody's thing to have a token hippie in the church. You had to have one there to show that your church was alive. Too often the church's concept was not, "These are hurting people and we need to move in and begin to touch them." Rather, though we'd never admit it, our motivation was that having a hippie

25

in the congregation made us look good in the light of the latest fad.

In charismatic circles some years ago, the fad was to have a highly cross-denominational gathering. If you weren't a part of a trans-denominational meeting, you really weren't with it. Episcopalian priests and Catholic priests and nuns had to be a part of any gathering. The black suit and collar or the habit said something. In many cases these people did have great things to say. But just because a man wears clerical garb, it does not follow that he is going to have a word from God for my congregation. But it was the fad, and there was pressure to get on the circuit and have these people in order to be with the in-group.

For a time many churches got into demonism, and it became very faddish to find demons and cast them out. Specialty ministries were being shipped all over the country to handle all these demons that were jumping on people. I received treatises on smog demons, cough demons, asthma demons, you name it. Everything was a demon.

Not coincidentally, the secular culture was on a big occult kick at the same time. Hollywood was producing *Rosemary's Baby* and *The Exorcist*. Fortune-tellers were capturing newspaper headlines around the country, and Bishop Pike was talking to his dead son on "the other side."

The demon fad in the churches was in response to this occult boom in the culture. I believe some thought needs to be given to the church's response patterns to world situations. Generally the church's reaction is exactly that—a reaction, rather than a prophetic life-style. We tend to take what the world is doing, put different wrappings on it, use emotionally charged religious terms, and sell it. We are very concerned about being "relevant" and we are not so concerned about being prophetic.

A good illustration now is the gay lib movement. What is the church's response to that? It's quite possible that this could evolve into a fad. Then, unless you have your resident gay or ex-gay group, you will not really be where the action is.

I'm not concerned about being "relevant" in that sense. I want to be prophetic. This means that I should be speaking what God is speaking. The gift of prophecy is a gift of insight. I should be bringing God's insight into situations.

What if Jesus were living in our country now? How would He deal with the cultural pressures we face? He said, "As the Father speaks, I speak. I simply see what the Father is doing and I do it" (see John 5:17). That is being prophetic.

We must begin to see what Christ is seeing and respond accordingly. He didn't start a political movement. In fact He shunned politics. Yet He was involved politically, not from a movement point of view but because what He did had fantastic political implications.

The prophetic life-style is person oriented. To deal with homosexuality in a faddish way would be to deal with the issue of gay rights. I'm not primarily concerned about that as an issue. First, I am concerned with a person who is caught in a life-style, being led to believe that he can never change, when the truth is he can change, Jesus wants him to change, and a host of people who have changed prove it can be done.

If I am to live prophetically, I must get to the individual. Making public statements won't accomplish the task. That only provides an occasion for others to voice an alternative viewpoint. Soon, all we're doing is firing back and forth at each other. I don't think the church should get into that kind of conflict.

To live prophetically in the world is to speak Christ's love and redemptive power into the heart of the individuals caught in sin. We see Jesus doing this. He didn't speak generally to the world but He did confront individuals—He touched this sick person, He released that demon-possessed person, He forgave the other person who was a notorious sinner.

Something potentially helpful that can become faddish in its application is the church growth and renewal movement. Certainly it can be helpful to observe what happens when churches begin to grow, but church growth does not basically depend on methodology. The dynamic for church growth is Spirit-filled people meeting other people's needs in Jesus' name wherever they are. You can't reduce that to methodology.

There's a great run now to get your buses, get your evangelism program, get on TV. You begin simply by going to the people who are doing it, and you make their counsel the voice of God. The church leadership goes to a seminar, comes back and says, "Folks, we heard the mind of God. We've got to buy 17 buses." Even if that seems to work, it doesn't necessarily mean that was God's word to you.

Just now there is great interest in an enormous church in Korea pastored by a Dr. Cho. What Pastor Cho is doing is absolutely profound and is impacting his country's culture tremendously. If you could observe his ministry from a solid philosophical base, it might be tremendously helpful. There might be something the Lord would want to reveal to you that you can't see until you go there. But if you go into that from a philosophical vacuum, you are just going to come home and try to duplicate it. We'll have little "Cho-ites" running around all over the place, being ineffective and tremendously frustrated.

There are many pastors seminars now. Pastors are flying all over the world trying to find "the key." That can have value if these pastors have their philosophical base. If they don't, it will reduce to faddism. Five years from now, all they will be doing is looking for the going thing again.

Traditional Ways

Those of us who belong to a denomination, particularly a denomination with many years of history and well-developed worship traditions, are likely to subscribe to a concept of church life that was simply handed down to us.

If we are isolated from others, living within the context of monologue so far as church life goes, we will probably accept uncritically many practices which have no validity. Or if they are valid, we don't know why and therefore cannot use them to best advantage. And we are totally unaware of alternatives that might suit our particular situation much better.

A superficial exposure to new forms won't do any good either. What's needed is a change in the basic pattern of being bound by tradition.

Unless you want to be aggressive, unless you want to be current in the true sense of the word, you can use "in" terms such as "body life" or "New Testament life" and simply inject them into your existing traditional flow. You are not changing at all. You are only superimposing new semantics on old patterns of operation. You still have not thought through a basic philosophy for your church.

Do you ever ask, "Why are we saying the Apostles' Creed?"

"Why this hymn?"

"Why hymns at all?"

29

"What is the application of church life out in the street, and how can what we are doing inside affect life out there?"

"Is worship an event that takes place, or is it a lifestyle?"

The beginning point for developing a philosophy is to really want to know where you are going, and to have the courage to do some basic self-evaluation. People often see worship as a means to an end. Is that how you see it? I don't believe worship is a means. It is an accomplishment in itself. The Father is seeking people who will worship Him in spirit and in truth.

People see sermons as vehicular. The preacher is going to say some things so that at the end he can insert a hook and draw people in the direction he wants them to go—to salvation, to commitment, to support of the building program, to start family worship, or whatever. The sermon becomes a vehicle to get the hook in the fish.

I don't view preaching that way. The Bible says we speak as the oracles of God (see 1 Pet. 4:11), which means that speaking itself is the ministry; preaching is to be oracular, not vehicular. As Jesus put it, "The words I have spoken to you are spirit and they are life" (John 6:63).

A pastor's speaking in and of itself should be used of the Spirit to accomplish ministry. As a pastor speaks, people should be saved, changed, edified. That is how it worked with Peter. "While Peter was still speaking these words, the Holy Spirit came on all who heard the message" (Acts 10:44). It worked this way with Jesus too. As He spoke, people were healed and changed. When He finished speaking, there was no need to hang around and pray. The work was done.

What I am saying is that we should not see valid forms

of ministry as vehicles to something else. For example, often music in the services is seen strictly as a vehicle. We have a sanctuary choir which sets the mood for the sermon which sets the mood for the hook. We do all this setting of the mood. No wonder when our people hit the marketplace it's inconceivable to them that they could say five words and strike the heart of a person with a direct message from God. They think the prospect has to be set up first.

Not only does very little happen in the marketplace because of such thinking but, also, despite all this fantastic setting-up in the church services, nothing much happens there either. What we should seek is valid ministry in each thing that comprises a meeting. While the choir is singing, something should be happening among the people. "All of these must be done for the strengthening of the church" (1 Cor. 14:26).

Nothing I have said about the dangers of traditional forms should be understood to imply that form is unimportant or undesirable. In the Old Testament, it was only after everything was finished in minute detail according to the prescribed pattern that the glory of God came into the Tabernacle (see Exod. 40:34). It is inconceivable to me that form should be thrown out and we be totally unstructured. I need some kind of form within which to operate. My whole life needs to be orderly. Our forms give order to what we do. What I'm saying is, don't worship the form. Don't be captive to it.

Principles, Not Specifics

Every church needs a solid philosophical base upon which to build its life and ministry. I have not given that to you in this chapter. I hope to outline such a philosophy in the remainder of this book, particularly in the chapter that follows this one. But remember, we will be

31

talking about basic principles and not about specific practices as such. The principles, if they are sound, will work for anyone anywhere. My practices are for my specific situation, my community, my personality. Chances are they might not work well for you in your situation.

For example, I don't stand behind a pulpit when I preach. I sit on a high stool. No great principle is at stake here. I began to sit while preaching because my legs were tired. I did not, however, break with the pulpit tradition easily. I had always stood behind a pulpit and it had never even occurred to me that there might be an alternative. But my legs began to protest. I found myself preaching five times a Sunday and unable even to straighten my legs when it came time to get out of bed on Monday morning.

Finally, one of the brothers said, "Why don't you sit down while you preach?" I had never heard of that before. It sounded totally irreligious. Then he showed me from Scripture that Jesus sat and taught the people (see Matt. 26:55). "If Jesus could sit down and teach," he said, "you should be able to. Your sermons aren't quite as good, but otherwise it would be OK."

The next Sunday I sat on an old wooden kitchen stool. It felt so good to get off my feet. More than that, though, sitting down broke me loose from the grip of tradition, and unfettered the congregation as well. It got us moving in some very interesting directions. I have gotten quite used to sitting while I preach now. I tell audiences that if they feel someone should be standing while I preach to go ahead and stand.

But sitting while you preach is a specific, not a principle. I received a letter one day from a man who had attended a pastors conference at which I had spoken. He said that when he went home, he got rid of their song books. He threw out the pulpit. He brought in a stool to sit on while he preached. Then he said, "And brother, there's still nothing happening here!"

Nothing will happen anywhere just because people make some of my practices a fad. But things will happen when the Bible's principles are put into practice. We will search out some of those principles next.

The Church as a Force

A mother was distraught because her two little boys were behaving very badly, traumatizing their whole neighborhood. One day the mother went next door and began pouring out her woes to her neighbor. The neighbor offered a solution. She once had a similar problem with her little boy. She took him to a nearby Catholic church and made him confess to the priest. That took care of the problem.

The distraught mother decided to do the same thing. She marched her boys down to the Catholic church and turned them over to the priest. The priest took the first boy aside and said, "Young man, where is God?"

The little boy was petrified and didn't answer. The priest repeated the question. The little boy jumped up, ran from the priest, grabbed his brother, and said, "We've got to get out of here. They've lost God and they're trying to pin it on us."

Communication is a very interesting thing. I may

know exactly what I'm going to say but still not have the faintest idea what you're going to hear. That is one reason I want to relieve you right now of ever having to agree with me. Beside that, I don't speak as an authority. I'm simply a person trying to apply the significance of the Christian life and life-style in the arena where Jesus Christ has placed me.

With that in mind, let me ask you a question. *What is the church?*

You may not fully understand what I am going to say about the church. You may understand well enough but disagree. That is your privilege. But whether you like *my* answer or not, you ought to have a well-thought-out answer to that question.

I'm sure that thousands of Christian people have no satisfactory answer to that question. Neither do many pastors. I've talked with pastors all over this nation who have absolutely no concept of what the church is. They've never thought about it. Oh, they studied the subject in a class in college or seminary. They have a notebook someplace, and they accept the definition in the notebook, but they aren't quite sure what that is or what it implies.

Then they begin to walk into people's lives, handling crisis after crisis, hiring staff, forming organizations, building structures, accumulating money. And they still don't have the foggiest idea what the church is.

Christian people generally are as confused as their pastors. Many of them know only that the "churches" of their acquaintance are a far cry from what God intended. That's why literally millions of people who profess to be born-again Christians are more or less alienated from the organized church. We live in a society that is coming to tremendously encouraging conclusions about God and about Jesus Christ. However, the conclusions of that same society about the church are not encouraging.

That particular dichotomy bothers me. Why does our culture have one opinion of Jesus and an altogether different opinion of the church? The Bible teaches that the church is the Body of Christ (see Eph. 1:22,23). It says that "in this world we are like him" (1 John 4:17).

When people differentiate between the church and Christ, when they say, "We're going to write off the church but we surely do love and believe in Jesus," something is seriously wrong.

I believe that we in the churches need to face that situation and its implications. To the extent that we do so, the Holy Spirit can teach us how to restructure or conceive the church so that there is no great gap between the way we see the church in the world and the way we see Christ in the world.

Toward this end, I want to put before you two models of the church. One model I call the *church-as-a-field*, the other is the *church-as-a-force*.

The Church as a Field

Do you think of the church as an organized, corporate structure, located in the community at a specific address? Something to which you can direct people? Something identified, visible? Maybe with a steeple and maybe not, but a definitely located entity? That's a partial description of the church-as-a-field.

In the field concept, the organized church is where the people come to do the work of God. A farmer's field is where he plants his crops and does his work. Just so the field, as it relates to the church, is the arena in which the church does its work. Whatever is to be done by the church is done there.

This concept—that the field is where the work is done

37

—is crucial. You see, Jesus said, "The field is the world" (Matt. 13:38). From that it follows that the work of the church is to be done *in the world.* When we think that the believer's meeting place is where the work is to be done, we have departed from the concept Jesus originally established. Instead of the world being the field, we have made the church the field.

This concept of the church-as-a-field will determine or at least temper all that the church does. Let's consider how the "field" mentality affects the church in its emphasis, goals, ministry, and motivation. And then we'll consider some of the end results.

The following description may be something of a caricature. It may exaggerate some features. Few churches probably fit the description completely. But I think the description will strike pretty close to home for many.

What does the church-as-the-field emphasize? When we see the church building as the place where the work of God is to be done, we develop the kinds of emphases that will get people into that building.

First, we need a great deal of visibility. The church must be prominently located. People must see it and preferably should have to pass it daily enroute to school, work and shopping. After all, how will they ever get there if they don't know where it is? Not only must the church be very obvious, the leaders of the church must take on a very significant PR role. I'm not against public relations, but sometimes PR becomes one of the main things in this concept of the church. Because we have to become visible, the leadership—whether the pastor, the associate, or whoever—must get into the community primarily to bring visibility to the church.

Second, the happenings that take place in this building must be of such a nature that people will be attracted. Program and promotion become very important. A high-powered program and strong promotion, of course, demand a great deal of effort, money and organization. So the church's emphases become visibility, organization, program, and promotion. I'm not saying these are bad. I'm questioning their validity as priorities. These are the main emphases in this concept of the church. We give a great deal of attention to these things, because we see the building as the place where action is.

What goals does the church-as-the-field have? The goals of the church-as-a-field are defined in terms of numbers in attendance, of budget and of facility. Those things tend to make up our concept of success.

Of course the goals are flexible. If we are not reaching great numbers then we change our success semantics from quantity to quality. We're after a few good men. And we've handled the success problem.

Budget? Obviously, it takes money to run a church. But when this becomes our goal, we have seriously confused means and ends. When we operate the church in order to get money enough to operate the church, we shouldn't be too surprised that people write off the church as something which is opposed to Christ.

Facility is vitally important to the concept of the church-as-a-field because the only way to increase the field is by enlarging the facility. If you are going to do a great work for God and it's all within the building, then you must have an enormous building.

How does the church-as-a-field go about accomplishing its ministry? An interesting thing here is that it does not have an adequate description yet of what its ministry is. Its ministry so far is to get people into the building, because that is where the work of God is done.

This work, once the people are gathered, centers around a professional. If people are going to be prayed for then the professional is going to be the person who does it because he has the professional hands. And when there are more heads than his hands can take care of we add another professional. So now we have four hands instead of two. As the field increases we have more heads than four hands can handle, so we add another professional. And then we departmentalize the professional so that we have hands in every area of the members' lives. What we are doing is setting up a rather stringent kind of professional approach to ministry.

The second thing about this kind of ministry is that the arrows all go in. By that I mean the organization is endeavoring to pull people out of the culture into the church. Everything is designed to draw people. We have contests, prizes, and outreach campaigns. I heard of one church that gave away green stamps. At another, the pastor promised to swallow a live goldfish when attendance hit a certain number. Anything, just get them in. Because this is where the action is.

Ministry becomes a positional identity within the organization. That is, if you are going to minister you must be director of something or minister of something or associate something. You will have a title and a position within the organizational structure. As a result, the individual member is easily misled about the meaning of Christian service and is often reduced to a spectator. You see, once he's in the field, unless he wins a position he has little relevance except to help keep the machine going.

He keeps his seat occupied and invites his neighbors, but that's not fulfilling so he becomes a bit confused. Then he either grabs for power or drops out. Or he regresses into a support or nonsupport role of the pastor's program. A lot of pastoral opposition stems from this kind of frustration in people's lives.

What motivates the church-as-a-field? Basically, the motivation of the church-as-a-field is to get people in. That is called evangelism. Once you have them in you must keep them in because if you don't the field is going to shrink. So elaborate programs are designed to keep the people. This results in an enormous amount of programming. You had to program to get the people and now you have to program to keep them.

You also must get people serving the church. The reason this is absolutely necessary is that the church is the field. Therefore, if people are to serve the Lord at all, they are going to be doing it within the organization.

Very subtly, an interesting thing happens in our mentality if we are not careful. We begin to exploit people. We're reaching people, not because they are hurting, but because they can help us in our church endeavors. *Just think, if that man with all his money would get saved, what he could do for this church.* Or, *What a good testimony for our church if that notorious sinner were saved here.*

Suddenly the purity of our motives is eroded, and that's a very dangerous thing. It means that at some point we are going to start hurting people. People are going to get chewed up in the machine. At East Hill we pick up pieces of people who have been chewed up in religious machines. We pick them up by the basketful. People who have been hurt, who hate religion, hate the preacher, hate everything to do with the church package. Many of them have a real case.

It's not because anyone wants to hurt people. No pastor is in the ministry to hurt people. I've had pastors come and weep in my office, saying, "I like people. I want to help them. I've spent my life trying to help people, but it seems that at some point they get hurt." Often these pastors have been under such pressure to

41

make the machine hum that they have allowed the people to suffer.

When the church is the field we are also motivated to compete with family, school, television and the world. That is no small task, but we must do it. Why? Because we have to rip people away from other things and get them occupied with the church program.

Now, what are the dangers of this approach to church life? First, the pastoral role is distorted and misdirected. In evangelical churches, the pastor tends to become a superstar. Some men have the ability to carry that role well. Their platform manner magnetizes people. In personal relationships they exude charm and self-confidence. As administrators they rival the top executives in big business. But let's face it. There aren't many of that brand of cat around. True superstars are few and far between. The vast majority of pastors must live in frustration if they work in a situation that demands a superstar.

Under some ecclesiastical systems, the pastor tends to become a puppet instead of a star. He hasn't enough autonomy as a leader to take hold of things and make them happen. He has too many boards between him and what he wants to accomplish. So he becomes a political puppet, compromising everywhere and just trying to keep everybody happy. That's also frustrating.

Whether a pastor becomes a star or a puppet, he is being misdirected. His true role is to be neither of those. Rather he is to be an equipper of the saints.

Even more frightening than what happens to the pastor is what happens to the church. Again the tendency is to go in one of two directions. The end result is usually either mediocrity or subculturization.

Let's trace out how it works.

Notice, we're talking end results here. The church-as-a-field may show absolutely no marks of mediocrity at the beginning. To the contrary, there may be great first-generation excitement. That group of people on whom the church was founded are blessed of God. They are excited, things are moving, the budget's always met, the building is coming, new people are present every Sunday. Everyone is awake. Hallelujah!

But the second generation is different, and I am not referring to the children of the first generation. I'm talking about the second wave of people who make up a church after it is well established. The building is complete. The income is adequate. The organization is functioning. The church settles into what I call a second-generation compromise. Everyone is quite comfortable now. The church program is going along nicely. The time for personal sacrifice is past. The people sit back to enjoy the fruits of their labors—or the labors of the first generation.

The stage is set for third-generation mediocrity. Nothing much is happening anymore. Faces change as people and pastors come and go, but that's about it. Even desperate attempts to shake things up, to get moving again, have little effect. Pastors get discouraged and leave, or settle into mediocrity along with the church. They sort of retire early, so to speak, giving up hope of anything significant happening but sticking with the routine anyhow. It's a living.

God help the poor pastor who ends up with third-generation mediocrity. But frankly, I think that's where most pastors are. That's why they shuffle. They trade this pastorate and its mediocrity for that pastorate and its mediocrity. They get about a year-and-a-half honeymoon out of it and then start looking for another church. Mediocrity is always looking for a way out. Give some release and it may honeymoon with you for awhile. But it always has a way of settling back down if we **don't** change basic concepts.

The only hope is the rise of a new superstar who can capture the day and move us on to bigger and better things and lead us over the top for Jesus.

If the church-as-a-field does not end with mediocrity, it will end in subculturization. Or it may be both mediocre and subculturized. A subculture is a separate system within a system. It defines its own life-style, has its own speech, and tends to externalize its basic spiritual qualities. It develops its own community. When a church subculturizes, it becomes, as one writer put it, "an island of irrelevance in a sea of despair."

That is, I think, a great danger for the Christian church. I see great segments of the church going in that direction or already there. The tendency always is to establish a community in which there is uniformity. That way we don't have to worry about error or nonpredictability creeping in. So the church tends, on the wave of revival, to take the result of that revival and institutionalize it. Years later the institution remains, but the life is long gone.

We tried to go the subculture route at East Hill in the early days. We didn't know any better. We had a close-knit group of about 10 families, and our basic aim was to solve all our own problems, keep our group intact, and add to our little community.

We had visions of establishing a Christian commune. We never were able to pull it off because someone would always come in who didn't look as we did, didn't talk as we talked, and didn't give a hang about our little community. We were always having to convert these people to our community concept.

Finally we began to get the message. I was praying one day for the Lord to give me the community and the

Lord stopped me. "Never pray for that again," He said. "I am not going to give a community to you. Instead I want you to pray, 'Lord, give me to the community.'"

This was how I finally awoke to the fact that God didn't want us to be a separate subculture, He wanted us to penetrate every segment of the society in which He had placed us.

Jesus said, "You are the salt of the earth" (Matt. 5:13). Salt, to have any effect at all, must be mixed in with the substance which needs salt. Nobody but a collector sets up saltshakers and admires them. A subcultured church is like a saltshaker on display.

Whether the church-as-a-field leads to mediocrity on the one hand or to a Christian subculture on the other, the result is the same. The world concludes that religion may be OK for some but it's irrelevant to real life. And Christianity is just another irrelevant religion.

Obviously these are gross generalizations. But these are concepts one must work through to arrive at any adequate definition of the church.

The Church as a Force

The church is people, equipped to serve, meeting needs everywhere in Jesus' name.

Do not underestimate the preceding statement. That concept of the church will affect everything: the way the pastor preaches, the way the church is organized and promoted, the way the program develops, and the way the building is designed.

This concept of the church is so decisive that if you don't see it in the thoroughgoing context I have just suggested, you do not understand what I am saying.

Among other things, I'm saying that we need to direct the church away from professionalism and into the hands of people who do not know what they are doing.

I want to say from firsthand experience that this policy is both scary and at times utterly ridiculous, but always, in my mind, necessary.

As we did with the church-as-a-field, let's examine the emphases, goals, ministry, and motivation of the church as a force. And consider the results.

What does the church-as-a-force emphasize? In this concept of the church-as-a-force, the field is the world, as Jesus said. That is where the work is to be done. The emphases in the church-as-a-field model are visibility, organization, program and promotion. The church-as-a-force emphases are worship, training, and fellowship, because *these are the things that produce Spirit-filled people who can meet others' needs in Jesus' name.*

When our people gather on Sundays and on Thursdays, they are not the church at work. To attend services is not to serve the Lord. Services are for what we might call R and R, rest and restoration, and this includes worship and celebration. We get together, we sing, we clap, we praise God, worship, meet one another, talk about Jesus. We don't hear any profanity or dirty stories. It's tremendous. It's unadulterated fun and enjoyment in a pure, clean, loving environment.

When we meet, we read the Bible and the Lord speaks to us in various ways. Brothers and sisters more gifted than we in certain areas minister to us. We thoroughly enjoy it. We're healed. Our lives are changed. We receive tremendous blessings. Why? So that we can gather for a repeat performance on Thursday night because by then we'll need to be pumped up again?

No! The church is rested and restored at meetings so that they can work in the world all week long.

The church is at work right now. People are sitting in board meetings where they are employed. They are driving taxis and trucks and buses. They are meeting in council chambers, in the legislature, in commissioners' offices. They're teaching classes. They're milking cows. They're changing diapers. They are all over the community.

When we get together the next time, we'll share what's been going on. We'll rejoice together over our victories and pray about our needs. Some people are going to be present who were caught in that work of the church out in the world. They are going to begin to understand what Jesus' life-style is all about. It's a powerful thing.

We worship, we pray, we fellowship, we learn.

What goals do we set? The church-as-a-field has goals expressed in numbers, budget, and facility. The church-as-a-force has goals that are personal and individual: We want each member to come to *wholeness*, be *equipped*, and be *released* into the world to minister. Our basic assumption is that the Holy Spirit who fills the pastor can fill every believer to whom the pastor preaches. And each believer is potentially capable of ministering just as surely as the pastor is, though perhaps in a different way.

The role of a pastor is to help Christians start living in the light of the truth. Evangelical Christians tend to have a lot of religion in their hearts, a good bit in their heads, but not much in their feet. And Christianity that doesn't walk around in shoes isn't worth much. It has to walk in shoes, all kinds of shoes—sandals, boots, high heels, and suedes. It has to walk. The role of a pastor is to teach people how to get their Christianity to walk right. If we only teach them how to think Christianity and how to feel it, but not how to walk it, we are failing.

Most church members are content to watch the pastor walk. "Pastor made 435 calls this month!" And the poor pastor. He is chewing Rolaids. He's drinking Maalox. His cheeks are sunken. His face has a yellow pallor. And the people come on Sunday mornings and get upset because he doesn't feed them steak. The best he can do is serve a little warmed-over soup. He's been busy.

Do you follow me? It's not my job as pastor to minister to every need in the church. I don't intend to do that. My job is to teach everybody in the church how to minister.

The Bible says that pastors are supposed "to prepare God's people for works of service, so that the body of Christ may be built up" (Eph. 4:12). Take careful notice of this Scripture for it is foundational to the concept of the church-as-a-force.

Preparing God's people—that's my job, and that's a whole different ball game from doing the ministry myself. The church needs to place its members in a healing environment of love, acceptance and forgiveness. We must bring people to wholeness in such an environment, equip them, and then release them.

What is the ministry of the church-as-a-force? The automatic result of great healing is great outreach. As people come to wholeness, they minister. Other people are touched.

When the church is a force the ministry-by-professionals-only tendency of the church-as-a-field yields to a ministry by all the believers. Along with this comes an altering, even a dissolution, of the traditional lay-clergy role. That is easy to say but it's hard to do in an established church. People don't know how to let it happen. They don't know how to cope with a pastor who actually expects the people to carry on the ministry. They almost demand that the pastor do the work.

The breakdown of the clergy-layman distinction is also frightening for pastors. The pastor is losing his safety zone and he feels vulnerable. People know he is as human as anyone else, though he happens to be a pastor. That's very threatening to some men. They fear they will not be respected any longer, that their leadership capability will be impaired. Many men are even taught in seminary not to be friends with church members—to keep a "healthy distance" away from the people.

Pastors are in fact as human and fallible as anyone else. Why play charades then? What good is leadership that must depend on falsehood for its strength?

I do not believe in vertical relationships in the church. I do not believe in the emergence of an elite in the church. You see, I have no power over anyone simply by virtue of the fact that I am a pastor. The only way I can function as pastor in anyone's life is if he lets me. If he doesn't want me to, there is not a thing I can do. I have no power to make anyone bend.

I could threaten people. I could set up a system of political pressure. But as a pastor, I must make it one on one with people. In order to do that, I must be an authentic person. That means I must take the risk of being open and transparent.

Being open is scary. And in some fellowships it is downright risky, as James D. Mallory, Jr. describes:

> One time in a Sunday school class on love within the family, Betsy admitted she sometimes had hateful feelings toward me or the children. The other members of the class clearly were not used to such honesty and immediately hid behind a pious cloak, suggesting they should pray for poor Betsy, who obviously was in dire straits as a Christian.

Many are afraid to take the type of risk Betsy took because others might think they are not very good Christians if they admit some of the foolish things they do and the destructive thoughts and feelings they have.

Betsy's honesty in the class ultimately paid off, however, and others began to share some of their problems. They began to function as the body of Christ should function. They could pray honestly and specifically for each other.[1]

In the church-as-a-force there is a climate of love, acceptance and forgiveness. The pastor is not living a life of pretense as if he were somehow different and better than others. These two elements alone do much to make the church a healing fellowship in which our Betsys and everyone else can be real and open.

In the church-as-a-force the pastoral leadership is also constantly endeavoring to facilitate the ministry of the members. This means the pastor carefully avoids usurping that ministry. He does not do the work for the people but involves them in doing it themselves.

A man asked me to pray with him about his living situation. He lived in a large apartment complex and felt like Lot in Sodom because of the things going on there. He really wanted to move. Our church could have responded to this situation in a number of different ways. For one, we could have built and operated our own apartments. Financially, we could have handled that with no problem. We had already been approached with that proposal and had property on which to build. But that was not our choice. If we ever did build an apartment house, we would limit the percentage of Christians living in it.

However, I couldn't just say to that man, "No, I'm not

going to pray with you. Sit there and tough it out."

I said, "Listen, you are not there by accident. Let's begin to work and facilitate some ministry for you. Let's pray. Let's fast, and we'll see what the Lord says to us."

I soon discovered a lot of other people in our church were in similar circumstances. One Sunday night after service we gathered everyone who lived in apartments, a whole roomful of people. I said, "How many of you feel like you want to move?" Many raised their hands. I said, "Why don't we stop asking God for a place to move and start asking Him for a way to infect the place we live? How can we have such a case of Christianity that we become an epidemic?"

They just lit up. The first thing they wanted was for me to appoint a staff member to come and teach a Bible study at their places. I said, "No, I'm not about to do that. That's crazy. Why increase the staff? You live there. How many of you are filled with the Holy Spirit?"

Then they thought I was saying, "Go down by the pool every Sunday morning, set up a pulpit, open the Bible, and say 'hear ye, hear ye!'" I was not saying that at all.

"I'm simply saying to be open for business," I explained. "Now what does that mean to you?"

One fellow decided he should write out his testimony and post it on the bulletin board. He happened to be in charge of an apartment building for 400 adult students of Mt. Hood Community College. He had been a bartender a few months before.

He posted his testimony on the bulletin board, where all the messages are. He attached a note, "If you want to talk about this, see me, manager's apartment." A steady stream of people began coming to him.

Now wouldn't it be foolish to put that man on staff? Or hire someone else as minister of apartment evangelism? Ministry is people filled with the Holy Spirit meeting the needs of other people in Jesus' name.

What is the motivation of the church-as-a-force? What are we trying to accomplish? We are trying to bring healing to the whole man, to every area of a person's life. We are not out to use or exploit people, as is the temptation in the church-as-a-field.

The church-as-a-force becomes a healing agency in the community, not a place of refuge from the community. Nor is the church a competitor with the world. We don't want to compete but to change priorities so that family, school, vocation, entertainment and the rest take their proper place.

For example, one exciting thing we're developing now is the concept of parents and children spending 12 years or more together as a healing unit in the public school system. That, to me, is a fantastic alternative to starting our own schools. I'm not opposed to Christian schools, but that is not God's call to our particular church. I'm not against Christian colleges, but I think the believers who have had no Christian background should be the ones attending them. Christian people who have been in church all their lives ought to be the ones attending secular colleges.

We are not in the world to compete but to change priorities. I don't care whether every family in our church has a television set or several of them. I do care that they understand priorities enough to know when to turn the set on and off. And that doesn't come from me going through the TV guide with them each Sunday morning to give them the recommended programs or placing the approved programs in the church bulletin.

The church-as-a-force concept is not without potential dangers. Most pastors get nervous when the ministry is placed in the hands of nonprofessionals. Ordinary people start going off in all directions, witnessing, caring, praying for the sick and distressed. The pastor may not even know about everything that's going on and he may begin to feel that things are out of control.

In fact, things are out of control, but a pastor need not be intimidated by this. I've decided that if only what I can control is allowed to happen through our congregation, not much will happen.

In the church-as-a-force, the pastoral role is dynamic and in constant refinement. That is also threatening to some pastors. You see, as the church is developing the pastor's role is also developing within that context. I'm doing different things now than I did a year ago, and I never do arrive. I must keep on responding to what God is doing in the Body.

Another danger in the church-as-a-force is the confusion that arises because of nontraditional structures and patterns of action. People who come to us with the field mentality deeply ingrained do not understand us. We are always having to educate a new wave of people. In three years we went from under 500 to about 3,000 members. That gave us a big job to do in communicating the principles upon which our church is built.

Despite these and other possible dangers, the end results of the church-as-a-force are wonderful. The true pastoral function—to equip the saints for the work of the ministry—is preserved. That is vitally important for, according to Scripture, that is the only true function a pastor has. That's it. And as much as a pastor can dedicate himself to that single work, he is fulfilling his ministry.

Individual member ministry is also preserved under this model of the church, and that too is crucial. I've found that people get excited when they have a reason for being Christians other than getting out of hell.

People get bored just waiting for heaven. So what do they do? They start complaining, griping, gossiping. The reason they are bored is that they don't know what they are saved for. They know what they are saved *from* and what they are saved *to* but not what they are saved *for*.

Frankly, Christians get tired of hearing evangelistic sermons continually. Many pastors try to evangelize audiences made up of 99 percent Christians. "What if one sinner is there?" they ask. I reply that if one sinner is there and he can survive authentic praise and worship and fellowship, he is an amazing creature. If he can survive that, no sermon you can preach will get to him.

Too often we are caught preaching to a minority while the majority are sitting there bored to death and wondering, *What in the world am I doing here?* The only thing that can justify their coming is to bring a sinner with them. Then they can go home and say, "Well, I sure didn't get anything, but at least the pastor talked to my neighbor."

The greatest criticism people make of their pastor is not that he doesn't love them or care for them but that he is not feeding them. That is terrifying when, in fact, the total role of the pastor is to equip the saints to do the work of the ministry.

When the saints start doing the ministry, they get excited, and the church truly becomes a force for God in the world.

Note

1. James D. Mallory, Jr. and Stanley Baldwin, *The Kink and I* (Wheaton, IL: Victor Books, 1973). Used by permission.

four

People Equipped to Serve

A young woman named Jackie, a fairly new Christian, walked into a major discount store in Portland. As she passed through the prescription area she noticed a woman leaning on the counter, obviously very sick. Jackie felt an impulse to stop and pray with the woman, but she did what 90 percent of us would do and said to herself, "No, she would think I'm nuts."

Jackie did her shopping and on the way out passed the prescription counter again. The woman was now seated in a chair, still obviously very ill. And again Jackie was impressed, "Go, talk to her, pray with her."

Jackie started on out the door, but she just couldn't go. So she resigned herself to become the classic fool for Jesus. She went over, sat down beside the sick woman, took her by the hand and said, "I can see that you're quite sick and I don't want you to think I'm imposing, but I'm a Christian. Would you mind if I prayed for you?"

The woman began to weep. She said, "I've been sick for so long."

Jackie just held her hand and with eyes open said, "Lord Jesus, I know you love this lady, and I know you don't want her to be sick. Just because you love her, heal her and show her how much you care."

That was it. They exchanged phone numbers and Jackie went home.

The next day Jackie got a phone call from this woman asking her to come to the woman's house. Jackie went. The woman's husband had stayed home from work in order to meet Jackie. The prescription the woman got the day before was unopened on the kitchen table. The woman and her husband were both standing there weeping.

The woman said, "When I came home I went to bed and slept all night. You know, I haven't slept all night for years." With her particular sickness, she slept only for short periods and had to get up to take medication. Her husband thought she had died. He came in and awakened her to ask if she was OK. She said that she felt great.

He said, "Well, you haven't taken your medicine."

She said, "I know it, but I slept all night."

She then told her husband what happened at the shopping center. So he wanted to meet Jackie.

The people knew practically nothing about the gospel. Jackie explained to them the love of Jesus, how they could be free from their sin, how Jesus wants people well not only physically but on the inside. They both trusted in Jesus Christ.

Equipped in the Spirit

I believe Jackie's experience was an example of the gift of healing operating in the marketplace (literally, since it was at a shopping center). The gifts of the Spirit, as I understand them, are God's means of getting to men and meeting their needs through believers. I do not believe that spiritual gifts were meant primarily for the sanctuary. Some of them can operate there, that's fine. But many of them were primarily designed for the street.

A word of wisdom, for example, should not be needed in the Body of Christ. Why? Because we have the mind of Christ (see 1 Cor. 2:16). Yet, Christians all over the place are trying to get somebody's word for them. Everywhere I go someone asks, "Do you have a word for me?"

I say, "Yes, I have a word for you. Get into the Bible."

The Bible says that there are many different kinds of gifts but one Spirit (see 1 Cor. 12:4). The word gift here is *charisma*, which means an extension of grace. How is the grace of God extended in this world? Through these charismas, these gifts, these abilities. That's how we extend the grace of God. Do you realize that when you speak the wisdom of God to someone you are exercising a spiritual gift even though you do not realize it?

We sometimes seem to think that a trumpet should blow and a quivering voice should break forth, "Thus saith the Lord. OK, we're going to have a prophecy now." Can you imagine going out in public and doing that? Do you see anyone in the New Testament functioning that way in the exercise of the gift of prophecy? Not one. It's not there. Why bottle the gift of prophecy in a wineskin that won't work outside the sanctuary? And have it so frightening in the sanctuary that people not initiated into the club see it and run out scared half to death?

I believe in the gifts of the Spirit. But I do not believe King James English is the only language the Spirit knows or uses. Jesus didn't use that language when He was here on earth. He used the language of the day. Why should the Holy Spirit speak now in the language of four centuries ago?

I believe, in our conversations with people who are questioning and confused, we can prophesy or give a word of wisdom to that person and not even know the Spirit has used us. Later we think, *Wow, where did I get that insight? Where's my notebook; I should write that down.*

What happened? The life of the Spirit of Christ moved through us. It's the natural flow of Jesus' life extending God's grace into the world, bringing God to men.

To see spiritual gifts operating in the marketplace excites me. Suddenly I see Christianity working out where people live. You don't have to get them into a building. Afterward, when they do come in, you tell them what they've got and send them back out.

Christian people by and large don't know what gifts they have because they don't see them in action in the everyday world. They hear about gifts and perhaps see a display at a meeting, but they don't see the pastor or anyone else ministering in the marketplace. They see gifts being exercised only by professionals and in sanc-tuaried settings.

That concept has to be broken down. There is nothing that Jesus did when He walked on this earth that He cannot do through any Christian. But people don't know it, they don't know what to do about it, and they aren't trusted by the leadership to go ahead and get it done.

What I'm saying is this: *People who are filled with the Holy Spirit are already basically equipped for ministry.* What the church needs to do is help people to understand this truth, not mislead them into thinking they are somehow unqualified to serve.

Christianity is not difficult to communicate. It's simple. We make it hard by our extreme efforts. We give soul-winning courses that take eight weeks or eight months. This communicates to our people how difficult it is to win anyone to Christ.

As a result, Christians are scared to death to tell anybody about Jesus. They memorize every possible question any non-Christian could ask as well as the correct answers—they want to have all the bases covered. When they have done that we say they are equipped. They aren't equipped, they are incapacitated. We have them so intent on nailing people with the Bible, giving answers to them, that they forget there is a person there—hurting.

Maybe the correct answer does not help. Maybe what a friend or neighbor needs is a cup of coffee to drink and an arm around his shoulder. Someone to listen and care. Someone to exercise the greatest spiritual gift of all—love. It doesn't take a professional to love.

We call in experts from all over the country to teach about the Holy Spirit. This communicates to our people how difficult it is to be filled with the Spirit.

We hire evangelists from all over the world to come and conduct healing campaigns. This communicates that only an expert can minister healing.

We buy space in our local newspapers and say, "Come, hear the word of wisdom, the word of knowledge, and see the gifts of the Spirit in operation through this man." This communicates to our people that unless you are the kind of person who can be written up in the paper, the gifts of the Spirit will not operate in you effectively.

We have great deliverance crusades. Why? All one has to do to take power over the devil is to have more power than he has. Any believer filled with the Spirit has that. The name of Jesus is powerful in the mouth of a believer. It's not more powerful in my mouth than it is in the mouth of any other believer.

We make specialties out of ministry. We make Christian service difficult. The reason we make it so tough sometimes is to massage the ego of those who want to be specialists. I've seen specialty ministries come and go. God uses them, for He will use anything as much as He can, but the majority of the time they are raised up for the ego satisfaction of men.

The healing of the memories is an interesting ministry. It's a specialty. I believe there are old things in our lives that need to be healed, but I don't think we need to make a specialty of them. "If anyone is in Christ, he is a new creation; the old has gone, the new has come" (2 Cor. 5:17). Talking and praying with another Christian can help, but it doesn't take 175 sessions to do it. What did the Holy Spirit do before there was such a thing as the healing of the memory? He's been healing people and making them whole for a long time.

The leadership of the church has sinned against the Body of Christ by communicating to God's people that they are not fit to serve Him. I still remember the day when I had to get out of my chair in my office and fall flat on my face on the rug, asking God to forgive me, because He had showed me clearly that I would be held responsible for every ministry I stole from my people. And I had a list of them. I asked God to show me how to avoid that in the future.

I still fail sometimes. The pressure of wanting things to work is great. We want to go "over the top for Jesus." We have to be bigger this year than we were last year. But in the name of getting the job done, we must not take the ministry away from the people whom God intends to do it.

Confining the operation of spiritual gifts to the sanctuary or to professionals is consistent with the church-as-a-field mentality. But it is not consistent with the church-as-a-force. More important, it is not consistent with Scripture.

Equipped in the Word

We have said that people who are filled with the Holy Spirit are basically equipped for ministry. What they need beyond that is to be equipped in the Word. By that I don't mean they must learn the proof texts they can use to club sinners into submission. I mean they must learn the biblical principles which will make them what they ought to be as Christians.

Truth must be communicated to people, and that is accomplished primarily through simple, direct teaching of God's Word. The place to begin is to teach people who they are in Jesus—positional truth. Who am I? I'm more than simply a sinner saved. What does saved mean? What are the implications of that? Ephesians is great on this.

Once a person begins to understand who he is and what he has, he will try the concepts out. When this process gets under way, the pastor will have to run to keep up with the people instead of always trying to cook up some way to get them moving.

I am convinced that pure, raw, direct exposure to the Word of God will absolutely change people's lives. In fact, many pastors would do their congregations a favor if they would stop trying to preach, sit down, open the Bible, and read it aloud. You can bet that 90 percent of the people aren't reading it for themselves.

We did a phenomenal thing in our services—we read the book of Revelation. The book of Revelation had just about bombed me out. I was so tired of charts. Yet it says, "Blessed is the one who reads the words of this prophecy, and blessed are those who hear it and take to heart what is written in it" (Rev. 1:3). It does not say, "Blessed is he who understands it all or figures it out a little better than the next guy."

I had found that the first book the typical newborn child of God wants to read is Revelation. I often thought, *The dirty devil wants to get him confused.* One day another thought barged in. *Don't you think that desire may be born of the Holy Spirit?*

"Lord, why on earth would you take a newborn baby to the book of Revelation—with its beasts and creepies and weird stuff?" I protested.

In the midst of that little exchange, the Lord said, "I want you to read the book of Revelation to your congregation, and don't you dare do an exposition on it." The only thing I was allowed to do besides read was to define terminology so that we understood what the Scripture was saying. That's all. No expository explanation of any kind, no charts, no books, no dates, no numerology, no cross-references, and no theorizing.

We spent six weeks as a congregation reading the book of Revelation every Sunday evening. The place was packed. I almost felt guilty for not preaching. We would read and read, laugh and weep and wonder. We did not learn who the Antichrist is. We did not date the Rapture. We did not get into the tribulation and millennium controversies. I have a position on those issues, but who cares? I rather think we are all going to be saying on the way up, "Wait a minute; this isn't supposed to happen now. My chart says so and so."

The Lord will just wink at Gabriel and say, "See there, I told them they wouldn't know the time but they didn't believe me."

I tell you, I don't think any of our prophecy experts

62

have it figured out right. If one of them did happen to stumble onto the exact plan, I wouldn't be surprised if the Lord changed things a little, just so that guy wouldn't have all eternity to brag about it.

We simply read Revelation. When we got through, we had a phenomenal concept of the *power of Jesus,* of the *sovereignty of God,* of the *security that is ours* on this planet, and of the utter, complete, unquestionable *triumph of the church* of Jesus Christ. On that last night the congregation stood together with uplifted hands and praised the Lord for nearly half an hour. I've never seen anything so powerful in all my life. I thought, *That's why the Lord takes new Christians to the book of Revelation. What does a new Christian need to know more than those four things?* Most preachers have so garbaged up the book of Revelation that they have nearly lost the whole thing.

We read through the book of Acts the same way. We read the book of James. I can't preach James. It would beat the people to death. I tried it. The most I could cover preaching through the book of James was about four or five verses and people were bloody all over the floor. I said, "Oh, man, we've got to call this thing off. James is nailing us to the wall." I don't need to preach the book of James. I just read it and the Holy Spirit clouts people; it's a heavy book.

My primary emphasis in teaching is to life-relate the Word. To do that, I must be immersed in the Word. I must live it. Its principles have to be mine. To this end, as a minimum I read the book of Psalms, the book of Proverbs, and the entire New Testament every 30 days.

That sounds like a lot of reading, but it is actually only 10-14 pages a day, depending on your Bible. It takes an average of a half hour a day, the equivalent of one TV newscast or situation comedy. It is so simple to cover an enormous amount of Scripture that way. Do it every 30 days and what happens? The Word gets worked into your system. You are being immersed in biblical content. Then you add to your reading whatever you want from the Old Testament and other books.

Added to my daily systematic exposure to the Word are my times of extended study. Once every two months, or at least every three months, I take two to four days totally away from my situation. I grab some orange juice and take off for the hills where there's no telephone and nothing can bother me. I can't stand to eat my cooking, so I just don't worry about food. It's not a big fasting thing for me. I like orange juice so I take a couple of bottles of that—and immerse myself in the Word.

All I take to read is a Bible and a linguistic help—a Greek testament and lexicon perhaps. I take no commentaries. I don't want my thinking restricted nor my preaching to be just a revamp of someone else's ideas. A lot of pastors would save time and energy for everyone concerned if they'd just buy their people commentaries and tell them what page to read each Sunday instead of going the sermon route.

At the other extreme from pastors who parrot one another are those who knock themselves out trying to be creative and original. These pastors sometimes fall into sensationalism or strange far-out interpretations of Scripture. The fastest and most valid way to originality is to be oneself. You see, I am an original (and so are you). As I "forgive" myself for being as I am, as I learn to trust God's good judgment in creating me as He did and begin to accept myself, I am original. I can't help it. God has put my brain together and tutored it so that no one else can pick up the Word and see exactly what I see in it.

Good preaching is opening the Word and communicating to the people what we see. That's all it is. I do not need to be quotable. I'm not interested in being quotable. I want my preaching to be walkable.

"All Scripture is God-breathed and is useful for teaching, rebuking, correcting and training in righteousness, so that the man of God may be thoroughly equipped for every good work" (2 Tim. 3:16,17). That's what I'm about—equipping the saints to work. And there is no way to do that but through teaching the Word.

Released to Minister

Our church was at one time very small. I sat around in my office reading and looking busy and hoping something would happen. Some of the concepts of the church-as-a-force had begun to penetrate my mind. I realized that the New Testament teaches that believers are to carry forth the ministry, but I didn't understand how I could get from where I was to where I should be in that regard.

A phone call came one day from a woman who had been a Christian for only two or three weeks. She said, "I've been talking to my neighbor and she wants to receive Christ. Could you come and talk to her?"

I said sure, walked out and got in my car and started down the road. I had gone no more than five or six blocks when the Lord began to speak to me. I knew in a flash what He was saying: "If you go there I will honor my word and on the basis of her trust in me that woman will be saved, but I will hold you responsible for stealing the reward of one of my sheep."

I said, "I don't understand that. She is going to get saved and I am going to be judged?"

It didn't make sense. Nevertheless, the Lord's word to me was so strong and so definite that I knew I couldn't go. I turned around and went back to my office.

On the way back I got a short but intensive course in pastor-people relations. I remembered a deep-sea fishing trip my wife Barbara and I had taken recently. She had tied into a shark out there—a big dude about eight feet long. She was having a ball trying to play out that shark. About that time one of the crew members came, took her pole from her and landed the shark for her. What a letdown. He had taken away her victory, and she resented it.

The Lord said, "Jerry, that's exactly what you've been doing as a pastor. You have been running in, taking away the ministry of the people, thinking you're doing them a favor. But I'm going to judge you for stealing their rewards." It was heavy.

Having Faith in the Gospel

I called the woman on the phone and told her I couldn't come, and I told her why.

She said, "But I don't know what to do. I don't know what to say."

I said, "Do you know Jesus?"

"Well, yes."

"If you know someone, you can introduce that person to anyone, can't you? What happened when you were introduced to Jesus? Were any Scriptures used? You could use those same verses if you want to. But just introduce your neighbor to Jesus the same way you were introduced to Him. If it worked for you it will work for her."

She agreed to try it, and we had prayer together on the phone. Less than an hour later, there came a knock on my study door. Here stood this woman and her neighbor, both glowing as if they had strobe lights on their faces. Not only had the neighbor been gloriously saved, but both women had begun to understand that leading people to Christ is not the exclusive work of a few well-trained professionals. Any Christian can do it.

In fact, the gospel is so simple that even a non-Christian can lead another person to Christ. I've known it to happen. A man who has been a member of our church for a number of years was a former drug pusher. He was led to Christ in a free love commune in downtown Portland. A girl from a Spokane commune and this guy were smoking dope together. One day he said to her, "I'd like to be free of this dope."

She was not a Christian but had been raised in a Christian home. She said to him, "I know how you can do that. If you trusted in Jesus as your Saviour, He would deliver you."

He said, "What? What does all that mean?"

She said, "I'm not going to tell you."

"Why not?"

"Because then you'll take off and be a Christian and I won't see you anymore."

He kept prodding her until finally she said, "All right, I'll tell you." She quoted John 3:16 and explained to him how to be saved. He went into the other room, prayed to receive Christ, and was delivered. He walked out of that place and never went back. She stayed and as far as I know is not a Christian to this day. This girl wasn't saved, didn't want to be saved, and didn't want him to be saved. Yet she was able to tell the way of salvation and the power of the gospel saved a man.

You see, the power is in the gospel, not in the presentation or the delivery. Paul said, "I am not ashamed of the gospel, because it is the power of God for the salvation of everyone who believes" (Rom. 1:16).

Do you see what our problem is? We who represent the gospel don't have enough faith in its power to believe what Paul said about it. Incredible!

Trusting the Life of Christ in People

Besides lacking faith in the gospel, there is among us a tragic distrust of the life of Christ in other believers. We are scared to death they are going to goof things up, whether through incompetence or moral or spiritual failure. So we don't release them to minister.

When it comes to incompetence, true, believers do sometimes goof. This sort of failure is not limited to the untrained, however, though it may be more prevalent there. But fail or not, we must delegate ministry to people because that is God's plan.

If I give away ministry to a brother and he makes a mistake, we can clean it up together. That's all right. I make a few mistakes along the way too. The only people who don't make mistakes are those who never do anything. We've had enough of those people in the church in the past. They don't make the church a force.

God is big enough even to turn our goofs into something positive. I believe the Holy Spirit sees to it that the mistakes believers make in sincerely seeking to serve Him are not fatal to His Kingdom or fatal to other people. We can trust Him.

Some pastors won't let the people minister because they feel it compromises the excellence of the church's program. Nobody else does the job well enough, so the pastor or some other trained professional must do it himself.

An example might be having a nice-looking bulletin. Should the pastor prepare the bulletin himself to guarantee that it looks good enough not to reflect adversely on the church? The pastor with a church-as-a-force mentality realizes there is a prior question to answer before that one. Why even have a bulletin? Do we really need it? A church of 50 people who see each other about seven times a week anyhow does not need a bulletin. We make a production of these things simply because they have been around so long. We almost think it wouldn't be church if we didn't have a bulletin. Nonsense. The only time a church needs a bulletin is when there are so many people that communication cannot be effective without some such vehicle.

But assuming your church needs a bulletin, what about the sloppy work problem? First, let's examine motives here. I believe much of the reticence of pastors to give ministry away traces back to an ego problem. We say we are concerned about the reflection on Christ resulting from mediocre work. That's the spiritual way to put it. I think what we're really concerned about often is the reflection on us.

The fact is that nobody really wants to do sloppy work. We need to train people to do their tasks well. But to say they are untrainable, that no one can do it well enough but us, seems clearly to be an ego problem.

One pastor was such an organized perfectionist that his daughter remarked, "Even his parties have to have four points and a conclusion." Guess who had to produce the bulletin in that church.

It all comes back to our basic purpose. Are we out to produce professional-looking bulletins and flawless performances? Or are we committed to producing people who can minister for Christ and who are actually involved in doing it?

If we are building people, we have to let them learn by doing. And we can't be jumping in all the time and taking the pole from their hands lest they lose the fish. We cannot insulate people from possible embarrassment and defeat because to do so is also to deny them the thrill of victory, the satisfaction of a task well done, the privilege of saying, "And I did it all myself."

You see, the measure of our success as a church is not necessarily how many people we have but what is happening to those who are there, whether they be few or many. Every pastor needs to ask himself, "Where do I want the people in my congregation to be in their personal development one year from now, five years from now?" Then he can work toward something far more meaningful than having a slick Sunday bulletin or a well-oiled machine. He can work toward what God has called him to do: perfect the saints.

Besides a basic mistrust of people's competence, I think I also see among many Christians a tragic mistrust of the life of Christ in His people so far as their moral and spiritual commitment is involved. Some seem to think we must put all kinds of hedges around Christians to keep them on the "straight and narrow."

I don't understand that. My people *don't want to sin*. They love Jesus and they are trying to follow Him, just as I love Him and try to follow Him. My people don't need a warden to guard them; they need a shepherd to guide them. And when they do sin, they need love, acceptance and forgiveness, not suspicion and rejection.

Pastors ought to be building the confidence of the people in the life of Christ within them, not tearing it down.

One brother who had not been a Christian long came

to me and asked me to pray that he would find a different job. "The place I work is so rotten you wouldn't believe it," he said. "I hear nothing but foul language and dirty stories, and there's not one other Christian there as far as I can tell."

I said, "I can't pray for you to get a different job. Why would I pray for God to take the only source of light out of a dark place? That's crazy. Why do you think God leaves us here on earth after we're saved anyhow?"

"I never thought of it that way," he said. "Do you really think ... ? "

"Here's what I will do," I said. "I'll join in prayer with you. I want you to call me every morning before you go to work and we'll pray together that God will keep your light shining down there."

For two weeks he called me and we prayed together every morning. Then he stopped calling. A week later I saw him and said, "Hey, I'm missing my wake-up call."

He said, "Listen, since we started praying, three of the guys at work have come to know Christ and I go down early so we can have a Bible study together before work. I don't need to call you, but just keep praying."

I said, "OK, now you'll probably get your new job. God has a core of light there now and I wouldn't be a bit surprised if you got transferred to another place that's just as rotten as this one was when you started."

The life of Christ is incredibly tenacious in a believer, and we need to trust it more. I'm sure someone could tell stories on the other side—how believers were drawn away by evil surroundings. That's where the fellowship of the believers comes in. That's what the collective gathering of the Body is for—to restore and strengthen one another. But that restoration and strengthening is so that we can then go back out as lights into the world, not so that we can stay insulated and isolated.

Seeing the Church as His Church

Not only do we fail to trust the life of Christ in other believers, but we tend to forget whose church it is.

The first year I was in the ministry, I became very frustrated. The church was growing and I was getting the credit, but I knew there was not the slightest relationship between what was happening and what I was doing. I felt utterly useless and completely irrelevant. And I was. I could have dropped in a hole and God's work would have gone right on. Probably a little better.

The latter part of that year I landed in the hospital. I was 27 years old, had prepared for the ministry for nine years and, after less than a year of pastoring, I was in the hospital on a heart machine and there was some question whether I could even continue pastoring.

My ministry, so-called, had lasted less than 12 months and been totally ineffective. I was lying on one of those dollies they use to wheel people around the hospital. I said, "Lord, I don't understand. I'm still in debt up to my gills for nine years of education. I did what I thought you wanted me to do. But none of it makes any sense."

Then this question came to me: "Jerry, whose church is it?"

I knew the answer to that. I'd been ordained and called. It was my church. That was my answer. Sometimes when I give the Lord a wrong answer I know right away that it's wrong. Not that God hits me or anything. There's just a divine silence that says, "That was really absurd." This was one of those times.

The Lord miraculously intervened in my life and in my health at that time. He restored me completely physically. I was back in my office in three weeks. There the question came again: "Whose church is it, Jerry?"

A passage from Ephesians 1 came to mind. It brought

74

me suddenly alive for it said the church "is his body, the fullness of him who fills everything in every way" (v. 23). I had the answer. It was His church, His Body.

Then I went to the Gospels and read Peter's great confession: "You are the Christ, the Son of the living God." Jesus answered, "On that rock [upon that confession of God-revealed faith in Me], I will build *my* church, and the gates of Hades will not overcome it" (see Matt. 16:16-18).

I saw what had been happening. What I had built, the gates of Hades had overcome. It was gone. What God had built was standing. I understood that Jesus builds His church, that I not only don't have to build it but cannot build it. That was what had given me trouble. I'd been under the tremendous pressure of having to build a church.

The Lord said, "It's my church, Jerry; I'll build it."

"Well, Lord, then what am I for?"

"Just hang around and do what I tell you," He said. "Just be available . . . and try to stay out of the way."

Since it's not my church and I don't have to build it, I also don't have to assume a lordship role over the people in it. I can release them to serve Christ. Like me, they simply need to be available to the One who is Lord of the church. That's all. They don't have to perform. They don't have to conform either. And they don't have to become a part of some organized outreach program.

Releasing the People to Minister

Releasing people to minister means setting them free to meet other people's needs whenever and however they can. There doesn't have to be a hook in their ministry that will get the sinner inside the four walls of our meeting place.

Let's be clear about this. Ministering is not inviting

75

people to church services. Inviting people to services is called inviting people to services. Ministry is serving people.

No doubt you know people who hate church but need love. Why would you ever invite such a person to church? What possible sense does it make to invite people who hate church to come to church? Give them what they need—love. Love with no strings attached. If someone is sick, he doesn't need an invitation to church. He needs a believer to pray for his healing.

I personally feel it's unethical to try to con a person into church, to make a friend out of someone so that you can make a convert out of him, to lure people into church so we can look good and compete with the church down the street. We are not in competition with anyone. And we don't need any underhanded methods that misrepresent who we are or what we are trying to do.

Every touch we have in the life of another person ought to be an authentic touch. You see, the reason we have tried so hard to get people into the church building is that we want to get them and God together and we have imagined that is the way to do it. At least that is the best reason. At times our motives aren't that pure.

But even when our motives are pure in this regard, our methods and concepts are often wrong. We have been more religious than Christian. Religion, precisely defined, is man's effort to please God. Any human system designed to reach and please any god is properly called a religion. Christianity is not a religion because its focus is not on man reaching God but on the reverse. God reaches out to man in the person of Jesus Christ.

When we try to get men to God, then, we have things backward. We are being religious instead of being Christian. That, to me, is a profound difference.

I call it the Immanuel principle. Regarding Jesus' birth we read, "The virgin will be with child and will give birth to a son, and they will call him Immanuel which means 'God with us' " (Matt. 1:23). Jesus was literally Immanuel; He was God with us. He came to us where we were and brought God to us.

That is Christianity—bringing God to people where they are. That means we don't have to get people someplace; all we need to do is get to them. When we reach out and touch them, God does.

That's not egotistical, that's Christian. "God was reconciling the world to himself in Christ" (2 Cor. 5:19). And what did Christ say about us? "As the Father has sent me, I am sending you" (John 20:21). That means that through the power of the Holy Spirit, we can bring God to man just as Jesus did.

What did Jesus do when He was here? He healed people, many of whom, incidentally, never even thanked Him. He taught people. He loved them. He shared His life with them. He showed them what they could be. He gave them direction. He put up with their failings and patiently showed them the better way.

Some people responded to Jesus and some did not. Those who responded to His touch were saved. And He is working exactly the same way today through His people.

That's exciting because it means we don't have to wait for the community to come to church. Many pastors are trying to get the community into the church. I cannot conceive of that. How am I going to get a million people into my church? But I can conceive of getting the church into the community. That's a simple matter. Just let the people go. They touch every cultural strata and they can plant seeds that will produce life.

But we must not encourage them to con people or

exploit them. Our world has been exploited to death. Everybody wants something, is working an angle, has a package of goods to sell. Freely we have received from Christ; freely let us give. Just give, no strings attached. Love people where they are. If they never come to your church, love them.

Another release we need to give the people of God relates to the way they witness. Pastors have sometimes harangued their people not to be ashamed of Jesus but to tell everyone they meet about Him.

I don't believe Christians are ashamed of Jesus. Those I know are glad to be identified with Him. What sometimes keeps them quiet is not shame but a God-given respect for the rights and integrity of the other person. In situations that are unnerving and unnatural, they don't want to start preaching. And they are absolutely right about that. There is a sense of propriety deep within people, and even in the name of Jesus they don't feel right about violating that. Unfortunately, because of the harangues or other pressures, they sometimes do violate their sense of propriety, and almost always that sort of "witnessing" misfires.

We simply need to be natural and real. If Jesus is a real person in my life, I won't be around you too long before you begin to know that. And one way you know it is because I'm showing God's love toward you, not because I'm preaching at you. We must plainly and simply love people.

Then evangelism becomes a serendipity. The word serendipity comes from one of Aesop's fables. The three princes of Serendip set out to find, under commission from their king, certain things of enormous wealth and value. While passing through the land seeking these things, they continually found little treasures to take along, though these things were not what they originally sought. These "incidentals" later proved to be worth more than what they had wanted in the beginning. Any valuable thing we encounter almost unexpectedly along the way is called a serendipity.

Evangelism is a serendipity. It just happens along the way for Christians who are living the Immanuel principle. I can't stop people from coming to Christ in our congregation now. I don't have to do anything to directly promote evangelism. It just happens.

How do sheep bear lambs? I've never seen a manual written for sheep on how to bear lambs. It wouldn't do a ewe any good if she could read it. Just get a healthy ewe in the right situation and she'll have a lamb. It will happen naturally.

Evangelism is like that. When people learn who they are in Christ and get released to minister, they will minister. It's the most exciting thing in the world.

six

The Families of the Force

Some time ago the Lord began to deal with me about a wrong attitude I had. I hesitate to say He *spoke* to me lest you get the idea I hear voices. When the Holy Spirit communicates with me, it is seldom if ever verbally. Instead I experience a sudden awareness. It is like a hunch or impression, except that it comes with a unique conviction that marks it as being not of my own invention.

Such an awareness takes much longer to communicate verbally than it originally took to understand. Anyhow, in this instance, the insight progressed something like this:

"Jerry, why don't you pastor the whole church?"

"What do you mean, Lord? I thought I was doing a pretty good job."

"Give me the names of 10 kids in your church, the little ones under age 6."

I named my three, and that was it. I suddenly realized that I was not pastoring the children. I didn't know their names. They bothered me. They made noise when I wanted to make noise.

I began to notice how our adults related to the children. When an introduction was made, it would be "I'm Joe and this is my wife Sue." Often a child was standing there, unintroduced, ignored.

I noticed how differently we treated adults. When children ran in the church building, we grabbed them and told them, "Stop it! Be reverent." When adults ran in the church building, we assumed there was an emergency and got out of the way. Is it possible for a child to have an emergency? Double standard.

We were communicating to the children, "You are not important. Christianity is an adult thing." It was that very attitude that prompted Jesus to rebuke His disciples. He told them to let little children come to Him. He taught that the way we treat our children reflects on our relationship with Him, no matter what we may think of our own spiritual brilliance (see Matt. 18:1-6; 19:13,14).

I was heartsick when I realized my error. I didn't love the children. They were a pain in the neck to me. I asked God to forgive me and to give me love for the children. I began to get down on my knees and talk to them face to face or lift them up to me. I began to ask their names.

I preached a series of messages on offending our children. The Bible says it is better that a rock be put about your neck and you be thrown into the sea than to offend one of these little ones. Isn't that incredible?

I believe the church of Jesus Christ, wholesale, has offended little children. That is why we often do not enjoy the blessing of God as we could, because there is

82

a millstone around our necks. Our church has experienced a new release of life, joy, faith, and ministry since we asked God to cut the millstone off our neck and to keep us from offending our children.

You see, the battered child is now a problem worldwide. Parents mistreat their own children. This is clearly the work of Satan, who "comes only to steal and kill and destroy" (John 10:10). But there is more than one way to abuse a child. We who would never batter a child must be careful that we in no way partake of the malevolent spirit of the evil one toward them. We need to reflect the love of Jesus for the children instead.

The last couple of years the Lord has really opened my heart to kids. Picture a little girl with her front teeth missing. Sally is sitting near the front at a Sunday morning service. She comes up to me, grabs my hand, pulls me down to her level and says, "Good morning, Pastor; how are you?"

"Fine," I say.

"I want to give you a kiss."

"OK, give it to me."

She does. Then I ask her how she's doing and, "Do you love Jesus?"

"Yes, and I'm going to serve Jesus all my life."

Then we have a little prayer together.

Sally doesn't have a father. Her mother has been divorced three times, and the girl is less than six years old. I didn't know all that at one time. She was just another kid in the church.

Billy came up to me and said, "Pastor, when I grow up I want to be a preacher just like you."

"Really? Why?"

"Because I love you."

In our church, we don't separate our people by age all the time. We mix them all together. We don't see the

83

children as the church of tomorrow—they are the church of right now. Praise is perfected in the mouth of a child.

Not only does the Father welcome the praise of children but also He wants the church to minister to them, especially to the many who are hurting and fragmented because of the tragic splintering of their homes and families. This is a ministry a "child" may need even after he or she is grown.

The Big Children
Debbie at 22 was still desperately in need of being loved by a family. Her alcoholic father and her mother separated when she was small. By fourth grade she could not respond to affection and had an ulcer. By sixth grade she was an orphan. A grandmother and an uncle raised her after that, but "our family took little interest in one another," Debbie says. "I had no sense of belonging to a family, much less being a significant part of one."

Even after becoming a Christian, Debbie longed for the sense of belonging to a regular family. Then it happened. A couple at East Hill with eight children invited her to come live with them. The result? "Because of my upbringing, I didn't understand the meaning of words like love and forgiveness and acceptance and giving and trust, but God, through this family, has given life to those words. I have been entirely embraced with my shortcomings and positive qualities alike. How much more then must God accept and embrace me? Now I know—really know—the meaning of those words."

Like Debbie, many other "big children" need the experience of living in a normal family. Runaways, rejected young people, prostitutes, unwed mothers, battered wives—more and more people bear the handicap of a poor family background. A few, like Debbie, have been "adopted" into wholesome Christian families. That's good, and we are encouraging our people to do more of it. An even greater priority to me, however, is the development of wholesome family relationships in the church. We want to be in the business of preventing situations like Debbie's, not only trying to heal them.

When Love Rules the Home

The environment of the Christian home, like that of the church, should be one of love, acceptance and forgiveness. People need these three things to come to wholeness and they need them in the home just as much as in the church.

We can have these three ingredients in full measure in our homes only as Jesus Christ is Lord both of the husband and the wife. I am not saying that to put down those who live in divided homes. I don't want anyone to despair. But just as a home is not complete with only a father or mother, neither can love be complete with only one parent being obedient to God.

My purpose is to advocate what God intended the home to be—a place where both husband and wife are under the total Lordship of Jesus Christ. I must warn you that if you are compromising your own commitment to the Lord, if you aren't in the process of becoming what He wants you to be personally, you are heading your home toward disaster.

People come to us with incredible marriage and family disasters. They come from every walk of life, high income and low income and everything in between. Usually the disaster is a result of husband or wife or both not being under the Lordship of Christ. If Jesus isn't your Lord, you must begin there to bring love, acceptance and forgiveness into your home.

"God has *poured* out his love [agape] into our hearts."

How? "By the Holy Spirit" (see Rom. 5:5). If Jesus Christ is not your Lord, if the Holy Spirit is not filling your life, you do not have *agape* love. You can fake it. You can have friendship and you can have emotional love, but just as you can't buy apples at an auto parts store you can't get *agape* anywhere but from God. He is the exclusive source.

Agape love must become the mark of our homes. "Husbands, love your wives, just as Christ loved the church and gave himself up for her" (Eph. 5:25). There it is again, *agape* joined with giving. *Agape* is always a giving love.

Do you know what an ideal marriage is? It is husband and wife each giving to the other all of the time. If both are giving, obviously both are getting as well, but the dynamic is completely different. I know a relationship is in trouble whenever a husband or wife says to me, "I am not getting anything out of this marriage." Apparently his or her partner is not giving anywhere near 100 percent, and husband or wife doesn't have an attitude of giving either, but is focusing on getting.

Love gives and it gives with the idea of meeting the other person's needs, emotional and spiritual as well as physical. One of the greatest love gifts you can give your partner in marriage is total, unqualified *acceptance*. You see, although I speak of love, acceptance and forgiveness as three distinct things, they are closely related.

It comes as something of a shock to most of us when we discover we didn't marry a saint after all. We married a sinner like ourselves. Acceptance means we give each other enough elbow room to live. Acceptance conveys the idea: "You don't have to be my ideal; I love you." This is real unqualified acceptance of you as you now are and does not imply, "I will accept you in spite of your obvious faults." That idea is egotistical.

Too often we act so as to communicate: "You are not exactly what I would like you to be." We compare here, suggest there, manipulate elsewhere, con a little, play little reward games. Why? We are not the Lord, and no one has to answer to us, including our spouses.

If you have a very capable husband or wife, beware of getting into competition. I was intimidated by my wife's grade point average when we were in college ages ago. Barbara was always disciplined, got her assignments in on time, made A's on the tests. I was always playing Ping-Pong or softball or basketball, drinking Cokes and running around. I could never figure out why she had a better GPA than I did. I was intimidated by her grades and I was intimidated by her discipline.

Years later, she launched her "Touch of Beauty" radio broadcasts. Way down inside of me there lurked a subtle fear that she would do better than I. Sure enough, that which I feared came upon me. Men would come up to me and say, "We listen to your wife every day on the radio." Competition.

God helped me realize that we are not in competition, that we can release one another to be what God wants each of us to be. Now, as I am writing this book, her first book, *How to Raise Good Kids*, is already out and doing very well. I can honestly say that I am not threatened by that fact. I accept her strengths now. They don't intimidate me any longer. I also accept her weaknesses and she does the same for me.

Accept your spouse; that is the greatest gift you can ever give him or her. If you have trouble with this, perhaps it is because at some subtle point you have not been able to accept yourself. In turn, that may be because you are not thoroughly convinced that God accepts you.

I lived a lot of my life trying to get God to accept me.

I didn't like me very well. I was too short. My ears were too big. I wasn't put together the way I thought best.

I was crossing the street in Seattle one day when the Lord spoke to me clearly, "Jerry, why don't you quit trying to be a Christian? You are one. You are accepted in the Beloved." I did not even know that last phrase was in the Bible.

Three days later, I was lying on my bed in the room I was renting near the college. I opened my Bible to Ephesians, chapter 1, and began reading. When I reached the sixth verse, it jumped on me like a thing alive—I am "accepted in the beloved" *(KJV)*.

That experience totally changed my life. Suddenly I wasn't trying to get God to like me anymore. He had liked me all the time. As I began to accept myself because God accepted me, I found I was better able to accept other people. So you see, acceptance, like love, depends on a right relationship with God which includes exercising the faith to believe that God loves and accepts us in Christ.

Along with love and acceptance, forgiveness is one of the most healing elements in a home or church. Now, forgiveness involves forgetting. We have not truly forgiven someone until that matter is dismissed by us not to be retained anymore.

People tend to retain grievances, and although they "forgive" they keep things in a little bag for instant recall as needed. Introduce that system into a home and it becomes absolutely devastating. One cannot live with a person who is collecting his mistakes in a little bundle and bringing them up periodically just to show him he is not nearly as smart as he thinks, because remember when . . .

"There we go again; I thought that was settled."

"Well, it is, but . . . "

When people live together in the same home, their weaknesses are going to show. They just will. A strong relationship is not one in which the people have no weaknesses but it is one in which each knows how to handle in love the other's failings.

In a marriage, people so often get into little ego struggles. A minor issue—leaving a rake in the yard, being late for an appointment, not putting gas in the car—becomes a major issue. Then it becomes a matter of, "You're always doing something stupid or irresponsible." We generalize from a small issue into a great accusation and we are caught in an ego struggle.

The classic example is the huge, enormous problem that arises when he squeezes the toothpaste tube in the middle and she rolls it from the end. All they would need to do is buy two tubes of toothpaste, let him squeeze all he wants and her roll to her heart's content. That would take care of it.

Such conflicts can be funny to hear about but they hurt when you are caught in one. Multiply the hurt by many repetitions and many other small issues and you come up with two people who love each other but have lost each other. They no longer communicate.

Many such couples find each other only in their children. That is their one meeting point. When those children are gone, the husband and wife separate or spend the rest of their lives together but alienated.

Couples can build an environment in which they will not lose each other if they will let love and acceptance rule the home. And if they will learn a few things about forgiveness. "Bear with each other and forgive whatever grievances you may have against one another. Forgive as the Lord forgave you" (Col. 3:13). Has Christ forgiven you? Then that is your basis for forgiving others. As a Christian, you have no excuse to be unforgiving in any relationship, particularly in your home. Forgive.

I must emphasize the importance of forgiveness not just as an event but as an environment.

"I forgave him for that thing."

Not good enough. You must forgive him for everything, all the time. People need the security of knowing they can blow it and still be loved and totally forgiven with nothing held over their heads. I am pleading for an environment of forgiveness in our homes, where people don't have to wonder or endure some painful interlude before they can be forgiven.

That is the kind of home I need. Not that I intend to offend. I am not asking for license. I am not asking to be a tyrant and still be loved. I don't want to be unreasonable. I don't want to be hard to live with. Not many men do, though it may look that way.

Sometimes I meet a person who seems to want to be hard to live with. I think, *He must be trying to be ornery, because he is certainly succeeding.* When I get close to him I find a frustrated person who can't understand why there is trouble and why people have a hard time with him. I don't know any woman who tries to be contentious either. I know several who have succeeded, but none who planned it that way.

We need to build an environment in which husbands and wives understand that their mates are not holding grudges against them, not remembering the mistakes of the past. I need to know that when my wife looks at me she's not screening me through all of the foolish things I have done over the past 15 years. And I've done a few, but I honestly think she has forgotten most of them. At least she has convinced me she has, and that is just as good. She doesn't throw the past up to me and I try not to throw the past up to her.

Forgiveness is liberating. If you don't have an environment of forgiveness you can't live freely. You can only defend yourself constantly. What chance do you have then? None whatever, because you are going to fail sometimes regardless.

I've seen husbands and wives live together as though they were vultures. He's perched over here and she's perched over there and they meet in an arena between. Each is just waiting for the other to make a mistake so he or she can lash out. Have you learned yet that people tend to live up to your expectations of them? Just perch there watching for your husband or wife to blow it again and you probably won't have to wait too long.

"My husband is never on time for anything," a woman said to me. "And he is always in a bad mood. He has never been able to handle money either." She went down a list of about 15 things her husband "always" or "never" did.

When she finished I said, "You undoubtedly have the most consistent husband I've ever heard of. You have been married for 24 years and this guy has made totally wrong decisions all that time—quite a record."

You get the point and so did she. What are you looking for? You will find it. If you are looking for a mistake you will find it, but a forgiving spirit does not look for mistakes. When the mistake is there anyhow, it forgives. This paves the way for continued living. Unforgiveness becomes a gate across your road of life. It drops down and you can't get through to go on. Only forgiveness can open that gate.

If you want a good home, build an environment that grows good homes. How do you have a good garden? Pull out the weeds and plant good seeds, not bad seeds. If you are planting seeds of rebellion, jealousy, suspicion, unforgiveness and criticism, what are you going to grow? You will reap what you sow.

To have a home in which love reigns, sow seeds of love. How do you do that? By being a loving person. You can be a loving person when Jesus Christ is Lord of your life and the Holy Spirit is shedding abroad the love of God in your heart.

What I'm saying about husbands and wives applies to parents and children as well. I know parents who are unforgiving toward their children. They remember every mistake that kid ever made. Parents whose children are grown and married tell me about the mistakes those kids made when they were still at home. Forgive your children. Forgive that teenager.

"But he hurt me."

Forgive it and forget it. Let the wound heal.

I'd like to inject into your home these three things—love, acceptance and forgiveness—but I can't. All I can do is point you to Jesus. He loves you, accepts you and forgives you. As you are exposed to His love, you can begin to love. As you realize His acceptance, you can begin to accept others. As you experience His forgiveness, you can forgive.

How many of your past sins does God remember? None whatever. There is no record of you in heaven as a sinner. Insofar as God is concerned, your life began clean when Jesus became your Lord. Bless God. That's strong. That's forgiveness. Put it to work in your home.

Learning the Christian Life-Style at Home

I am utterly convinced that most churches have not done a good job of teaching children the Word of God. We have taught them information, but we have not taught them life-style. The evidence of that is in the many sinners who know the Bible. They grew up in our Sunday Schools but they are living for the devil. They know the answers but they don't follow the Lord. The information they have; the life-style—no way.

Some time ago I decided I was through educating people to go out and be more knowledgeable sinners. It was simply impossible to go on that way. I didn't know how we could better teach life-style, but we began to search for a way. We looked all over the country, in vain, for churches that had resolved this dilemma. Few were even asking the same question in any urgent way. What could we do?

We went to the Bible. Our question: what principles can we find in Scripture and how can we implement them in a church of three or four thousand? We knew we faced an incredible task, but it had to be done. The first thing that became clear from the Scriptures is that home is the place and parents are the people when it comes to providing Christian nurture. The Old Testament established it and the New Testament affirms it (see Deut. 6:6,7; Eph. 6:4).

Our mentality, like that of many others, had been, "Families, support your local Sunday School." We began to see the distortion in that. Sunday School should support the family. If Sunday School had to shut down for six months to get families together again, it should do that.

Sunday School has been allowed to usurp the place of the home as an institution for the spiritual training of children. When that proves inadequate, we turn to the Christian day school. That doesn't work either. We have forgotten that children learn their values and their life-style at home. So the church must focus on the family as a unit. The family must not only become healthy in its environment but effective in its communication of Christian truth.

With these principles in mind, East Hill developed and launched a pilot program called Home Base. We are not yet ready to package and export the program, but we are encouraged with what is happening so far and have opened Home Base to the whole church.

Rick Boes, who coordinates the program, comments, "With programs in the past, parents have been able to sit back and let the church take responsibility for teaching their children. Home Base runs directly counter to that in that parents are taught to teach Christian principles at home. In addition, Home Base gets families together to share ideas. In this way, strong families can help weak ones."

It also works the other way around because we can all learn from one another when it comes to ways of communicating Christian truth in everyday family living.

The introduction of the Home Base program does not mean the abandonment of formal Christian education programs by the church. In fact, we want every member, each week, to have one corporate worship experience, one family learning experience, and one peer group experience. Home Base provides the family learning experience.

My Own Family First

We do not appeal to families to support the church and its programs. Instead, we structure the church and its programs to support the family. We believe the family unit is central in God's plan.

Now, it would not be very consistent of us to take the position I just stated and then have the leaders of the church sacrificing their own family life for the sake of the "work of the Lord." If a staff member comes to me with a family problem, I say, "What do you need? Do you need time away? Do you need to go walk on the beach awhile with your wife? What? Anything you need, we'll help." Then I send him home and tell him I don't want to see him back in his office until things are OK at home.

Not long ago an elder came to me and said his children were getting hard to control, his wife was edgy, and he was troubled about his family. I asked him how long he thought he needed and he said six months. I told him to take a year and get things under control. If things were OK before that, fine. But he had a year free from any duties. All the other elders prayed with him and blessed him. I'm glad to report he's making fine progress and will soon be able to function effectively in a position of leadership again.

My own family is extremely important to me and I take Monday every week to be with them. I am never available for anything else on Mondays, I don't care what it is. If you come to my house and knock on the door on a Monday, I will not answer it. I don't answer my phone. Only my secretary can reach me at an unlisted number, and that only in the most extreme circumstances.

I also set aside certain evenings for my family. Nothing violates that. Pressures of church business are never allowed to intrude. I consider that an act of love not only to God and my family but to the congregation. You see, I would have no ministry left if my home were to go.

It's not that we have just decided to emphasize the family throughout the life of the congregation. We didn't make that decision. God did. We're simply trying to listen to Him.

seven

Dealing with Difficulties

Have you found that you don't change easily? Many people change only under pressure. Not because they want to but because they must.

Nothing in human experience is a greater catalyst for change than pressure—usually the pressure of some sort of difficulty. Yet we ordinarily do all we can to avoid pressure situations. Non-pressured living has become almost a god in our world.

If you design a life free of pressures, you probably also will have a life of mediocrity. Count on it: without pressure there is little change, and without change there can be no growth.

As Dr. James D. Mallory puts it, "People seem to assume that conflict is inherently bad or that the ideal life would be one that is conflict free. Anybody that is conflict free, I would suspect, is not experiencing growth.... The important changes in us take place within the framework of struggle."[1]

Another James put it this way: "Is your life full of difficulties and temptations? Then be happy, for when the way is rough, your patience has a chance to grow. So let it grow, and don't try to squirm out of your problems. For when your patience is finally in full bloom, then you will be ready for anything, strong in character, full and complete" (Jas. 1:2-4, *TLB*).

Welcoming difficulties in the life of the church isn't easy. Yet every difficulty that arises there also presents an opportunity for growth, either for individual members or for the corporate body. The church's difficulties are either problems with people (the resolution of which should lead to personal growth) or problems with practice (the resolution of which should lead to corporate growth).

Problems with people tend to revolve around certain personality traits. Let's consider a few examples.

The Spirit of Criticism

Nothing can tear up a fellowship quicker than a spreading spirit of criticism. And nothing is more antipathetic to love, acceptance and forgiveness. The two attitudes cannot coexist.

In 1978 I was away from my church for about three weeks to hold a pastors conference in New Zealand. When I left home, the people at East Hill were concerned with loving one another and being filled with the Holy Spirit. I returned to find them upset, unhappy with one another and jabbing at one another.

The ladies ministries had sponsored a fashion show. As a part of the fashion show, one of the women had modeled a bikini. The local newspaper covered the fashion show and along with their article ran one picture.

You guessed it—a shot of the gal in the bikini. Some of our members were quite upset about this turn of events and were ripping into the model and the woman responsible for the fashion show.

The bikini had been only a small part (no pun intended) of the fashion show, which in turn was only a part of the program that night. In fact, through the testimonies and that entire program presented to some 500 women, several of them gave their lives to Christ. The newspaper had presented a positive write-up, praising the fashion show as one of the finest. And the bikini photo had been published without comment.

When all this landed in my lap on my return from New Zealand, I was upset. Not about the bikini. It's false to be upset about a bikini in a fashion show and not about the ones being worn at almost every swimming pool. Anyhow, only women were present and it would not have mattered to me if they had been modeling lingerie.

I could see some reason for concern over the picture in the paper but I was a whole lot more concerned that Christians were ripping Christians, and a spirit of criticism was replacing a spirit of love, acceptance and forgiveness.

I met privately with the woman who had modeled the bikini and the woman who set up the fashion show. I said, "There has been some objection to the content as you know. Most of the complaints have come from men, none of whom were present. But maybe they have a point. Maybe you need to evaluate your program, keeping in mind your weaker brothers. But no one is judging you. I'm backing you 100 percent, and that is what I'm telling those who come to me."

The women decided they would forego their rights and omit bikinis in the future; it was no big deal.

The more serious problem, the unloving criticism, called for action from me. I brought the whole situation out in the open in a service. I told the people that knowledge (in this case, knowledge of what should not be done and why) puffs up but love builds up, according to 1 Corinthians 8:1. I told them that they were responding to this situation below the level of their maturity in Christ. Love won the day, the critics saw their error, and the fellowship was restored.

If the women had actually done something wrong, I'd still have taken action against any critical spirit developing. If something is wrong, we simply acknowledge that it's wrong and pray that the devil won't be able to seize on it as a means of hurting people. We don't abet the devil's work by making or promoting attacks on the people involved. We talk with them, deal with the issue, and treat them with love, acceptance and forgiveness.

Quick to Take Offense

Sometimes people get offended with one another or they get offended at the pastor. These situations need immediate attention or they tend to get worse. Often the problem is spiritual in its origins. The Bible says, "Great peace have they which love thy law: and nothing shall offend them" (Ps. 119:165, *KJV*). A person who is easily offended apparently doesn't love God's law very much.

Offenses unresolved tend to harden into bitterness and to spread to other people. The individual believer who is offended should take steps to resolve the matter himself. He should "make every effort to live in peace with all men and to be holy; without holiness no one will see the Lord. See to it that no one misses the grace of God and that no bitter root grows up to cause trouble and defile many" (Heb. 12:14,15).

100

In the last analysis, an offended person must deal with the problem himself because if he chooses to be offended no solution imposed or no appeal from others can mollify him. As Scripture says, "An offended brother is more unyielding than a fortified city, and disputes are like the barred gates of a citadel" (Prov. 18:19).

About all we can do with people who are offended is appeal to them. We had a situation arise among our staff members. Three secretaries got miffed with one another and the staff pastor with whom they work was out of town. So it fell to me to do something. I called the three of them into my office and told them I was embarrassed to have to talk to people we had hired about this sort of thing. I said, "I don't care who is right or wrong. I don't want to know any details. This is not a trial, so you don't need to present your case. I only know that you are not relating as sisters in Christ.

"I'm going to leave the room. There's a half hour left in the day for you to get this thing ironed out. I want you to come out of here loving each other. I want you to pray with one another. I want you to forgive one another. I want each of you to call me tonight and tell me that is exactly what you have done." Then I left and went golfing.

They all called me that night. They had gotten things straightened out, and everything was right again. Praise God! Let's help one another to see that we are bigger people than to indulge in that kind of nonsense. Let's keep our relationships right, and then the right and wrong of issues that arise will work out.

I could have held court, attempting to judge right and wrong, but even if I had succeeded in that, these women still would not have liked one another. What good would I have done?

A woman in our congregation became offended at me

because I didn't visit her in the hospital while she was ill. She had been there seven days and was complaining to various ones that "nobody" visited her. We checked into it and discovered she had an average of four people a day visit her—28 visits in seven days from people in the church.

I called her at home and asked how she was feeling. "Well, I'm feeling fine . . . *now*," she said.

I said, "I understand you've been in the hospital."

"Well," she said, "it's a little bit late."

"A little late for what?"

"I was there for seven days, and nobody even came to visit."

I told her I understood she had visitors from the church every day. "Yes," she said, "people from the church came but you didn't come."

I said I knew that, but I figured all the other people who came to see her had the power of Jesus too, and that every person who walked into her room represented a visit from Jesus. Was it possible she had missed all those visits from Him because she was hung up on the personality of one man? I wanted her to see Jesus in her brothers and sisters, whether the pastor got there or not.

She said she had never looked at it quite like that, but she got the point. And she quit being offended.

Debate with Schismatics

"Avoid foolish controversies and genealogies and arguments and quarrels about the law, because these are unprofitable and useless. Warn a divisive person once, and then warn him a second time. After that, have nothing to do with him. You may be sure that such a man is warped and sinful; he is self-condemned" (Titus 3:9-11).

We are not to enter into debate with schismatics. Not

that there is no room for people of good faith to discuss or even disagree on issues. But if a person is habitually "gendering strifes" (see 2 Tim. 2:23), causing confusion, and sowing discord, he must not be allowed to continue.

You can identify a schismatic by the backwash in people's lives. He touches one person and that person becomes confused. He touches someone else and that one is angry with this one. In his wake the schismatic leaves all kinds of confusion and strife. He is a troublemaker.

Sometimes these people are not aware of what they are doing. They don't realize what effect they are having on people. That's why Scripture says to warn them once and again. I have had to go that far in dealing with a schismatic. In our second conversation, I said, "One of two things can happen now: you can stop it, or you can leave. You must decide whether your fellowship in this Body is of enough value to you to stop what you are doing and begin to relate rightly. You decide and I'll call you to learn what your decision is."

The person to whom I said that responded well. He really needed to get some things straightened out in his life. I referred him to a counselor who worked through his problems with him, and he was healed.

When I give a teaching, I don't demand that everyone agree with me. But I do demand that no one sows discord in the Body by campaigning for an opposing view.

Suppose, for example, that one of our teachers began to present some views that ran counter to what I was preaching from the platform. That teacher and I would have a conversation the very same week. If I detected a sincere desire in that teacher to get the truth across, we would discuss how to do that together. I would ask for his views and we would together seek a proper balance in our preaching and teaching. And we would set down certain policies governing our relationship. We would commit ourselves to support one another.

But if I detected a rebellious spirit in that teacher, I would confront that, for he would be playing the role of a schismatic. You see, one's attitude and motive is the issue. You can't work with a person who is "warped and sinful" and who won't repent.

The Traditionalist

When church-as-a-force principles are put into practice, some people become uncomfortable. They are used to the old ways and things don't seem quite right to them. Treat these people with understanding. It's one thing to shatter old traditions but quite another to shatter people. When we feel we need to do the first, we must be careful not to do the second in the process.

People come into our congregation because the life of the church appeals to them and draws them. After being with us awhile, they begin looking around for some of the things they were accustomed to seeing in other fellowships. One woman came to me and said, "Pastor, do you have a visitation program here in this church?"

I knew exactly what was happening. She was beginning to look around to see if we had the elements traditionally considered necessary to a live church. I said, "We certainly do. We have what is probably one of the best visitation programs of any church in the world."

She said, "You do? Really?"

I just knew the next step would be for her to draw from her purse a list of names of people the visitation committee should call on, so I paused only a moment.

"Yes, we do," I said, "and you're it."

She said, "What?"

I said, "You're it; you are the visitation committee." It turned out that she did have the list of names. I told her that if people came to her attention as needing a visit, they were automatically her assignment.

What a lot of lost motion we save by not channeling everything through a committee. Our visitation program has the simplest structure in the world: you see the need, you meet it.

People simply need to be instructed. Otherwise they become confused. They don't understand and they misinterpret what they see happening or not happening. In our church, a core of people who know what the church-as-a-force is all about communicate the principles to newer people as the need arises. We also have training sessions for new members, and that helps.

In addition to all kinds of problems that arise because of difficulties with people, every church faces problems because of difficulties with practice. One of the most common and most troublesome of such difficulties concerns the role of the pastor.

What Is a Pastor to Do?

I believe a pastor needs to focus his ministry where his strength is. That is, he needs to operate in the area of his gifts and calling. Most men, unlike Jesus, do not do all things well. This causes all sorts of complications.

Many churches play a variation of musical chairs with their pastors. Suppose a church has a pastor who is good at personal counseling and gives his energies to it. The preaching ministry is neglected as a result. When time comes to call a new pastor, the pressure is on to find a man who is strong in the pulpit. Sure enough, the next man preaches well but he is not a good administrator or he is not good at one-to-one relationships with people.

The problem is: How can a church provide a balanced ministry to the community with a pastor whose gifts and calling are limited?

If a pastor of limited abilities (and that's about all of us) pursues his specialty and lets other needed work go undone, the church comes out with a lopsided ministry. If he tries to do everything, the pastor comes out frustrated. Even the work he could have done well suffers because he is drained emotionally by trying to perform those tasks he cannot do well.

The only answer that makes sense to me is to employ more than one person to do the many tasks that too often fall to the pastor alone.

I know that this "only answer" will seem to be no answer at all to the smaller church that can hardly afford one salary, let alone many. But I've been there too. I've dusted pews and swept the church. A man's gifts and calling may be narrow but he can still perform a wide range of functions. And in a smaller church he almost has to do that. But he should be working all the time toward giving away everything that is peripheral to his own personal calling.

As staff is added to a church, the aim must be to release the pastor to his personal calling. As our church grew, I had to make a basic choice. Was I called to counsel, to administer, to communicate truth in the public teaching ministry, or what?

My calling was to teach. So we hired a counselor and we hired an administrator. As they added their strengths to mine, the needs of the church were more fully met and each of us was happier and more effective. A pastor's calling must always be kept in mind when staffing a church; you don't just go out and hire an "associate pastor."

Churches do better and pastors live longer when the man is mated to the task. I can preach three times on a Sunday morning and not be tired at all. I enjoy teaching seminars. I go home from teaching a seminar stronger than when I left. But let me counsel for a few hours and I'm worn out. It exhausts me. We have a man who can sit in his office seven days a week and counsel people. He can have appointments all day long and come out strong. He can't understand how I'm able to preach several times a day, and I can't understand how he can counsel all day every day.

Administration is the same way. I am impatient with details. I dream big dreams, set directions, make far-reaching decisions. It may take a whole department six months to work out all the details connected with implementing one basic decision. I can't handle that. If I had to herd all those details through the endless meetings required, I'd go crazy.

Our administrator can come out of one of those sessions and say to me, "Boy, we had a good business meeting."

I'll say to him, "There is no such thing!"

He comes out excited; I'm worn to a frazzle. That is why he is the administrator. That is his strength. He enjoys working out the details that transform a dream into a reality. Administrative people are responders, not directors. They take direction and then make things happen.

Now, on the other hand, if I were an administrator and the pastor of the church, I would seek to add staff in the area of Bible teaching and counseling. If I were a counselor, I would add administrative and teaching staff. Visitation? I don't see that as a staff function. Neither is evangelism. These are the people's ministries.

What Kind of Building Do We Need?

The question just considered, What is a pastor to do? was answered in part by the principles of the church-as-a-force. He is not to do the people's ministry for them.

107

Church-as-a-force principles can also tell you a lot about what sort of building you need.

Do you have the church-as-a-force concept well enough in mind yet to anticipate what I am going to say as to the first decision you need to make regarding facilities? It's simple. Before you can decide what kind of building you need, you must decide whether you need one at all.

"Oh, but of course a church must have a building." Really? Where is it written? I've been studying my Bible intensively for years and I still cannot find either a design for a church building or any statement that we should have one.

Before you can decide whether or not you need a building, you must know specifically why your church is in existence. What is your unique ministry to your community? Are you just there to be redundant?

What good are you if you are simply going to duplicate what some other church is already doing in the community? For example, is another church in your area having great success with a Christian day school, kindergarten through grade 12? That is no reason for you to rush in with a similar, competing program. In fact, it's good reason not to do so. Obviously whether or not your calling is to operate a school has a great bearing on what facilities you need to build.

Don't automatically assume you need to build anything. Perhaps your church should meet in homes, at a public school, in the armory, in a rented hall, at someone else's church building. Your own ill-conceived building could turn out to be a tremendous liability, locking you into a situation that will hinder rather than help you in accomplishing what God has in mind for you.

Suppose you do need to build. The first thing to remember is that you are not building a church but rather a place for the church to meet. The church is people, and the building must be constructed in such a way that it will serve the people. Don't allow a reversal of that in which the church becomes servant to the building. In other words, don't let the building limit you from doing what you want to do. Make sure it is functional and serves all your purposes.

Since the church is people, design a people-centered building. When people walk in they should sense the importance of people, not be diminished by the structure or overcome by a huge cross, window, chandelier, or whatever.

The church-as-a-force concepts applied to building can save a lot of money by deleting a lot of unnecessary and sometimes undesirable extras. How many things in the average church building are there simply because it's a church? Since the church is not the building, we're free from all of that.

When a person walks in the first thing he should see is another person. His eyes should not be drawn to the ceiling, the window, the platform or anywhere else. He should look at someone who will look right back at him, who will welcome him with a spirit of love and acceptance. Then he can begin to understand at once what the church is.

In the worship service, people need to see each other because they are worshiping together. They haven't come as spectators to watch the performers on the platform. The seating should be arranged in some semicircular pattern so that the people will not have to look only at the backs of other people's heads.

Since we haven't come to watch a superstar, the platform area will be simple and will be designed to bring the pastor close to the people. The sound system must also be mobile so that people can have the capability of participating from their places throughout the sanctuary.

In summary, if you need to build, spend sufficient time first in determining the features you need in order to accomplish your ministry. Then get professional people to tell you how to do it. Don't get some lone-duck contractor with a cheap idea of what a church should be. Get someone who knows what he is doing and can do it right. It will pay in the long run.

How Can a Big Church Stay Person-Centered?

I once believed that a congregation of about 300 persons was ideal. I thought a big church could not possibly meet the needs of its members and that whenever a church threatened to become too large it should branch out and start another church. Obviously I don't feel that way anymore. Today I think a church of 3,000 is not too large, nor is a church of 30,000 too large. I mean that, so let me explain why I feel that way.

When Peter preached on the Day of Pentecost, 3,000 people were converted then and there (see Acts 2:41). These people "devoted themselves to the apostles' teaching and to the fellowship, to the breaking of bread and to prayer" (v. 42).

In other words, there were more than 3,000 members in the church at Jerusalem in its beginning. The principles of church life were originally formed in and are designed for a congregation of thousands. And it is in a church of thousands that these principles may be expected to work best.

This is a concept we need to grasp because so many times we have a mental block about size. I had a tremendous barrier in my own mind in this regard. I simply could not believe that church life could be increased in its effectiveness, enjoyment and value to the individual as the numbers multiplied. But I found out it can.

When church life suffers in quality as the numbers increase, it is because the church has not adhered to New Testament principles—the concepts of the church-as-a-force, if you will.

The church-as-a-force is person-centered. If the big church stays person-centered, it will increase its effectiveness with its size. If it ceases to be person-centered, it will begin to die from within.

The big danger that confronts a growing church is institutionalism. Organizations are forever trying to usurp the place of people, to minister by committee, to structure and channel and control and direct and swallow up people. Institutionalism is so subtle and so pervasive that it creeps in without our realizing it. If we aren't watchful, the institution will continue to swell and the people will start to shrink, as far as church life is concerned.

One reason we get sucked into institutionalism is that we want predictability. Institutions are safe. They are manageable. They are the same today as they were yesterday. We know where to plug in and we know where to unplug. We like that sort of security. But it is deadly when we get caught up in a machine and forget that God's church is first, last, and always, people. Churches do not exist for the sake of the machine. They are not cogs in "something bigger and more important than the individual."

East Hill has a benevolence ministry. We give food and clothing to those who are in need. As a part of this, we operated a 17-acre collective farm. Our people marked it off in plots, grew gardens, and from them supplied various social agencies with food. Hundreds of pounds of potatoes as well as other vegetables were provided this way. It was beautiful.

The man who coordinated all of that came to one of our council meetings to request a doubling of funds for the program. His request was legitimate; he showed just how the funds would be used. Somehow something didn't seem right to me. I sensed a hesitation within and I said, "Wait, something is not right here; we need to table this for awhile and think about it."

What was wrong? Only one thing; we were beginning to institutionalize. We were getting everything centralized so that anyone who had goods to give put it in a pot. Then those who had needs were directed to the pot. We were training our people to say to a needy person, "Go on down to the benevolence office; they'll take care of you." This would replace, "Oh, you need help; I'd like to do something. We have some extra food. I have some clothes for your children, clothes my little ones have outgrown."

We were taking ministry away from the people, centralizing and institutionalizing it. And it was happening without our even realizing it. We were acting from the best of motives. We denied the budget increase. In fact, we cut out the entire program. I went to the congregation, told them about it, and said, "Now, you are the benevolence department of this church. It is up to you to order your lives so that you have resources available to meet people's needs."

True, our members won't get a tax break doing it that way. It won't show on their tithing record. So what? It is what we give in secret without thought of reward or recognition that most pleases God.

Difficulties—they never quit coming. By their very nature they are no fun. But they don't have to trouble us unduly either. We don't have to become cynics, murmuring, grumbling, feeling sorry for ourselves, and asking mournfully, "What next?"

112

If we have a solid philosophical base in the principles of the church-as-a-force, we can deal with difficulties and come out stronger in the process.

Note

1. James D. Mallory and Stanley Baldwin, *The Kink and I* (Wheaton, IL: Victor Books, 1973). Used by permission.

The Church as Servant

A radio station specializing in rock music offered the local churches in its area an opportunity to present a five-minute daily program. The pastors could preach as they saw fit but they were not to plug their own churches or give their church names and addresses. Not one pastor responded to this opportunity. Yet three of them bought time on another station so that they could be free to promote their own churches.

Serving Christ
I don't understand the mentality of Christians who feel that the interests of their own church must be served by everything they do, who won't serve the Lord Jesus Christ unless they can use it somehow to hook people for their own fellowship.

I heard some people talking at a seminar. One said,

"You know, I lived beside this neighbor for years. I talked to him, witnessed to him, invited him to services, told him about Jesus. When he finally began going to church, where do you suppose he went? To a Baptist church down the street!"

I said, "Praise the Lord!"

He said, "Praise the Lord? I did all the work." He felt his work was wasted because the neighbor went to a different church.

Others have said, with mournful tones and sad faces, "I'm afraid we've lost that family to the church down the street." That's no tragedy. If my daughter moves from one bedroom in our house to another, do I consider her lost to the family? Let people get into the "room" where they belong, settle down there, and grow. The name over the door doesn't matter much. What matters is that people are fed spiritually and then released back into the community to meet people's needs in Jesus' name.

East Hill is able to meet the needs of many different kinds of people. That is why they come. But we are not right for everybody. We are not the only legitimate fellowship of believers in our area. If someone chooses to attend another church, feels at home and grows in the faith there, I say praise the Lord.

We are here to serve Jesus Christ, not ourselves. The church that is a force for God doesn't stand around calculating what it has to gain whenever an opportunity to serve Christ arises. It is too busy responding to the opportunities.

Serving as Christ Served

The principles of the church as servant go deeper than I have so far suggested. Jesus said, "Even the Son of Man did not come to be served, but to serve, and to give his life as a ransom for many" (Mark 10:45). Much of the church has failed to come to terms with the basic principle behind those words. Even where the words have become familiar, even where they are often cited, they are usually applied only to relationships between Christians. We miss the truth that the church is to fill a servant role in the world, as Jesus did, serving not only the brotherhood but everyone. Paul wrote, "As we have opportunity, let us do good to *all people*, especially to those who belong to the family of believers" (Gal. 6:10, italics added).

To say that the church is in the world as a servant is also to say that we are here to give, not to get. We are here to give with no strings attached; to help people because they have a need and we have resources, not because we hope to gain something.

A Place to Be Healed

One of the greatest services a church can offer a community is to provide a place for people to be brought to wholeness—to be healed physically, spiritually and emotionally. A place where people are loved, accepted and forgiven.

People are fragmented. They are torn. Life doesn't work for them because they are without Jesus. They don't need more programs and more activities. They simply need a place to be healed. The place does not have to be fancy. The physical environment need not be impressive. The people don't have to be super-spiritual. They simply need to be real, loving, accepting, forgiving.

Ingrid was a high school girl who had blown her mind on acid. By the time she was a junior, she claimed she had been on 500 "trips." She was angry, rebellious, and alienated. She had no Christian background or training whatsoever. She had been kicked out of every class by her teachers at Gresham High.

Ingrid first came to East Hill with a friend of hers who made a pretense of following the Lord but soon bombed out. Ingrid would stand off in a corner, wearing a rumpled fatigue jacket, smelling like a garbage pit, and emanating hostility.

After she'd been hanging around like that for awhile, she began coming into my office to see me. Her visits were like nothing I'd ever experienced. She would simply sit on the floor and look at me, for what seemed like forever and actually was perhaps 10 or 15 minutes. Then she would get up and walk out without having said one word.

This continued for several days straight. There'd be a knock on my door, and in would come Ingrid to sit and watch me. I'd talk to her but would get no response, so I'd just continue with my work. After awhile she would get up and walk out. I sensed that something was happening in her life but I certainly didn't understand what.

Then one day, in the midst of one of these silent sessions, I looked over at Ingrid and she was crying softly. I said, "Do you want to talk?"

She said, "I need to receive Jesus," and poured out all the garbage of her life.

Ingrid did receive Jesus, and it was a rough road for her for awhile. She came off drugs and God began to restore her mind. She went to every one of her teachers at high school, apologized, and asked to retake her classes.

Her counselor at school called me and said, "I don't know what has happened to Ingrid, but she is a completely different girl."

We had to walk Ingrid through some things. She had an alcoholic father who beat her for coming to church services. Her mother was an extreme neurotic. It was a great day when "Ink" graduated with a high grade point average. She gave me the tassel from her cap and I still have it.

Meanwhile as God brought her to wholeness, Ink began to be burdened for other kids in trouble. She began to get acquainted with officials and chaplains in the correctional system and eventually took a job as a counselor in one of the state institutions. She shared her burden with others in the Body, and as a result we now have teams going each week into every correctional institution in Western Oregon, with 40-50 of our people actively involved.

Ink is now married with a child of her own, and she and her husband have dedicated themselves to helping troubled kids.

Other Ways to Serve

Providing a place where hurting people can be healed —we want that always to be our primary service to the community. That does not mean that we won't serve in other ways.

When Jesus fed the 5,000, He didn't make them promise to attend His preaching services as a condition for receiving aid. He didn't extract a doctrinal statement from people before He healed them. Nor did He go to them afterward and say, "Now, you owe me one." He wanted them to believe in Him. He wanted them to be saved. He wanted them to respond. But He healed them because they were sick; He did so knowing that some of them never would believe in Him as Saviour.

I realize that when Jesus fed the 5,000, He was fulfilling prophecy and giving evidence that He was the Messiah. He was the Bread from heaven who had been promised, prefigured in Moses and in the manna which fed the multitude in the wilderness. I know that when He healed the impotent man at the pool of Bethesda, He was providing a "sign" of His deity and He left a multitude of other sick people there untouched. His ministry was primarily a spiritual one and His Kingdom not of this world.

Does that mean He was merely using people? That when He worked a miracle, He cared nothing about individual suffering but only that a spiritual message get across or His messianic claims be authenticated?

To think such a thing distorts not only the character of our Lord Jesus but the Word of God as well. I wonder if that might be the reason Scripture records not one but two separate incidents of Jesus feeding the multitudes. You see, John's account of the feeding of the 5,000 clearly focuses on Jesus' fulfillment of the Mosaic prophecy (see John 6:14,30-51). But Mark's account of the feeding of the 4,000 just as clearly focuses on Jesus' compassion for the people (see Mark 8:1-3). Jesus was concerned about both His divine message and human need.

The church is in the world today as the Body of Christ to continue the work He began. As such we are to bear witness to His divine nature and mission, and we are also to show compassion to people in need. Why are we forever falling prey to the idea that we must be occupied with only one of these ministries or the other? Why can't we do both?

We believe the church must serve the community. Jesus said, "If you love those who love you, what credit is that to you? Even 'sinners' love those who love them. And if you do good to those who are good to you, what credit is that to you? Even 'sinners' do that. And if you lend to those from whom you expect repayment, what credit is that to you? Even 'sinners' lend to 'sinners,' expecting to be repaid in full. But love your enemies, do good to them, and lend to them without expecting to get anything back" (Luke 6:32-35).

"*Without expecting to get anything back.*" Those are key words. The *King James* puts it, "hoping for nothing again." You see, we are the people of God. That means we don't depend on this world system. We may use some of its vehicles, but we are not bound to it. We do not need its approval or support. God provides for us, and we are free to give, "hoping for nothing" in return.

Jesus said, "Freely you have received, freely give" (Matt. 10:8). That is the spirit in which the church must serve the world. It is true that Jesus also taught that those who give will receive abundantly, but we must not allow that to compromise the purity of our motives in giving. If we give, we will get, but we don't give in order to get—not if we obey Jesus. No, we give in order to give.

Helping the Public Schools

Among Christians these days there is great concern over the quality of education and the moral climate in our public schools, and rightly so. Private Christian schools have been promoted as a solution to the problem, and may be one alternative. However, that solution does nothing to help the public school. To the contrary, removing the Christians tends to abandon the public school system to its doom.

As we began to check into this issue, we learned that the average American family with three children is involved with elementary and secondary education over a period of some 20 years. That is the span of time from the day the oldest child enters school until the youngest graduates. That gives time for in-depth involvement.

We also learned that in any public school system,

parents can function on curriculum committees, on school boards, on advisory committees and in parent-teacher organizations. Actually, most public schools are crying for parental involvement and getting very little.

We discovered that few of our people knew both names of their child's teacher. Even fewer knew the principal's name. We couldn't find anyone who knew the superintendent's name. Few knew anything about the school board, and no one had ever served on a school board. Do you get the picture? Here we were crying about the public school but really behaving irresponsibly ourselves, doing nothing to improve the situation.

We decided to take a first step and simply get the parents, the children, and the school officials together for once. We learned several interesting things: (1) the school people wanted to talk with the parents but hadn't found adequate ways to do so; (2) the parents wanted to talk with the school people, but were afraid or didn't know how; (3) the children wanted their parents to be involved in their education and to know their teachers. The children felt totally segmented; they had a home life and a school life, and the two never met.

Our first parent-school workshop aroused so much interest that the state sent a delegation to observe whether this thing they had heard about was actually happening. They indicated that no church had taken on such a project before and they were amazed.

Christian teachers started coming out of the woodwork. In fact, we discovered a whole battery of Christians strategically placed throughout the school system. With Christian parents involved and Christians working throughout the system, why abandon the whole thing to the devil?

It's not that now we want to participate in the school

system in a manipulative sense. We don't want to take over anything. We want to serve the community by helping to make the public school more nearly what it ought to be.

A number of these workshops were conducted at our church. We brought the parents, children, and teachers together on age-graded levels. This gave them opportunity to know and understand one another better. Parents learned how the system works so they could be directly involved if the Lord led them that way.

We said to teachers and administrators, "We are Christian people. We want to know how we can, with intelligence and understanding, provide the kind of input we feel necessary in the formation of the educational program. We are a part of the community, and we want to be a responsible part."

Through such interaction, we helped to prepare cool, clear-eyed Christians who, when a moral issue comes up, do not grab their Bibles and start clubbing people but who intelligently respond, "As a parent, this is my view . . . I have a right to this view, and you must take it into account because I am representative of a part of the community."

Such a voice is all too seldom heard. Often we are so self-righteous in our reactions that we do not serve the cause of true righteousness well.

Better Homes and Gardens

A house in Portland's west hills burned down, and the man who lived there lost everything. He thought he was insured, but through some sort of slip-up, he was not, and he was wiped out financially.

The members of a nearby church, several of whom were carpenters and contractors, pitched in, took up offerings, supplied labor, and totally rebuilt his house, without a penny coming out of his pocket. They did it simply because they felt the Lord wanted them to do it. The man was not even a member of their church.

Utterly overwhelmed by such a show of kindness, the man was solidly converted to Christ. The people who helped him had not done so because they planned to convert him that way. They helped him because he had a need and they had the capability to meet that need. The impact on the neighborhood was profound. People still drive by to see the "house the Christians rebuilt."

Some of the men in our church helped a woman in a somewhat similar situation. She contracted to have some remodeling done on her home. The contractor took her money but did not finish the job, leaving one whole side of her house open to the weather.

The woman was contemplating going to court to sue the contractor. Our men said, "You are going to get pretty cold if you wait on a court action to settle this. On the other hand, if you get your house fixed, you will no longer need to go to court. So let's do it that way. We'll do the job, and you can forget the suit."

They didn't just shelter her from the weather, either. They finished that house beautifully. The result: not only was the grateful woman rescued from her predicament but the contractor was left scratching his head and trying to figure out just what kind of people these Christians were.

The Bible says that the believer is to "work, doing something useful with his own hands, that he may have something to share with those in need" (Eph. 4:28). "That he may have . . . to share." Don't miss that *sharing* part. We hear a lot of teaching these days about prosperity. Some of it gives the impression that if you are not driving a Cadillac or a Lincoln, something must be wrong with your faith. I believe God prospers His people, but the purpose is not to make us extravagant but to make us capable of ministry.

I've been to the highlands of New Guinea, where people live in abject poverty. One day my host took me into the countryside and said, "Pick out the Christians' gardens." I looked, and sure enough, the gardens of the believers were producing better than those of the non-believers. "We pray over our gardens," my host explained. "We want to grow enough food to share with our neighbors who cannot pray God's blessing on their gardens as we do."

I learned something about prosperity that day from some of the world's poorest people. I saw clearly how false it is to feel superior to others simply because one has more of this world's goods. What I am doing with my resources says infinitely more about my spiritual condition than does the fact that I have them.

A Child Will Live

I told earlier how the Lord dealt with me about my attitude toward the children of our congregation. That was good, that was a beginning. But what about the children in our nation and in other nations that don't have anyone to love them?

As that question burned in our hearts, Barbara and I were led to adopt an orphan from the land of India to be our fourth child and to live in our home. Through our opening our home and hearts that way, many other people in the congregation have been encouraged to do the same. I haven't been evangelistic about it. I haven't preached to the people that they should do this. I do not in fact believe that every family financially able to do so should adopt a child. Our doing so was a very personal thing with us, a responding in compassion to the needs of one suffering child.

As God led other members of our congregation to reach out to children in need, we saw them come into our church family in increasing numbers. Today I would guess that there are several hundred adopted children in our congregation. Some people have adopted whole families of children. One family has 13 adopted children, all of them in the "hard to place" category because of physical defects.

One of these children, also from India, was abandoned by his mother in a garbage can when he was five. She apparently counted on him crying loud enough for someone to rescue him. He was found and taken to an orphanage but not until he had been in there so long he was at the point of death, and his sister, in the same garbage can, was dead.

I have been asked, "What right do you have to arbitrarily select one child, out of the masses who are just as needy, and give that child all the benefits of your home while you do nothing for the others?"

I can't really answer that question, except to admit the injustice of it and to point out our need to live redemptively in an unjust world. I know that our taking one child is not going to mean much to the ones who are left in their suffering. But it is going to mean an awful lot to that one little boy.

You see, I can't bring about justice in this world. I have neither the resources nor the wisdom necessary. I could put myself under great condemnation because I eat well while children are starving. But what good would that do? Even if I reduced my family to a bare subsistence level, the world's poverty problem would remain virtually untouched.

But because I cannot live justly in the world, it does not follow that I should do nothing, that I should ignore human need and indulge all my resources on myself.

No, I am to live redemptively. I can touch this one here and that one there, and make all the difference in the world to that person.

That is what Jesus did when He was here among us in the flesh. He didn't bring in the Kingdom in the sense of banishing all hunger, sickness, and injustice. That glorious condition is yet to come. What He did do was touch an impotent man here and feed a hungry crowd there—and forgive the outcast sinner in yet another place. He lived redemptively.

I was still a kid in college when I first encountered real poverty. It wasn't in a foreign land either, but right here in our own country on a Navajo reservation in the Southwest. On the particular reservation I visited, 75 percent of the children had tuberculosis or would contract it by the age of 15. Many of them would die before they reached age 20. Few would ever get off the reservation.

I remember going into that situation and seeing kids and chickens everywhere—and dogs. The kids were dirty and hungry and I just wanted to put my arms around every one of them.

What do you do in a situation like that?

I took one little girl on my lap and hugged her. I couldn't embrace all of them. I reached out to one. I showed compassion where I could not bring justice and complete deliverance.

That is where we are in the world today. We face tremendous needs. We cannot rectify all the wrongs, lift all the burdens, heal all the sick, defend all the oppressed. But we can stop and bind up the wounds of one we encounter along the way, instead of passing by on the other side. Yes, and we can go out of our way as we are led by the Holy Spirit to do so in order to give a redemptive touch to someone.

Ending with a Comma

I have told various ones that this book will not end with a period. I cannot end it with a period, because it is an incomplete statement. I haven't given the final word on the church-as-a-force. I am still learning and following on to hear what the Lord has to say about living for Him as a body of believers on this planet.

No doubt the Lord has things to teach me that I do not yet sense even dimly. Even now He is saying new things to us about learning the Christian life-style, and about the use of our resources. So this is not the end of the story. It is, however, a place to stop, the place to write the closing "comma."